		DATE DUE		

Kranz 01-02 BHS 27.45 332.4

Straight Talk About Money

Marion Rendon and
Rachel Kranz

 **Facts On File**
New York • Oxford

Straight Talk About Money

Facts On File, Inc.
460 Park Avenue South
New York, NY 10016
USA

Facts On File Limited
c/o Roundhouse Publishing Ltd.
Oxford OX2 7SF
P.O. Box 140
United Kingdom

Library of Congress Cataloging-in-Publication Data
Rendon, Marion.
    Straight talk about money / Marion Rendon and Rachel Kranz.
        p. cm.
    Includes index.
    Summary: Discusses money, the economy, ways of earning and saving money, and its significance in society.
    ISBN 0-8160-2612-2 (acid-free paper)
    1. Money—Juvenile literature.   2. Saving and thrift—Juvenile literature.   3. Finance, Personal—Juvenile literature.   [1. Money. 2. Finance, Personal.]   I. Kranz, Rachel.   II. Title.
HG221.5.R46   1992
332.4—dc20   91-36586

A British CIP catalogue record for this book is available from the British Library.

Facts On File books are available at special discounts when purchased in bulk quantities for businesses, associations, institutions or sales promotions. Please call our Special Sales Department in New York at 212/683-2244 (dial 800/322-8755 except in NY, AK or HI) or in Oxford at 865/728399.

Text and jacket design by Catherine Hyman
Composition by Facts On File, Inc.
Manufactured by the Maple-Vail Book Manufacturing Group
Printed in the United States of America

10 9 8 7 6 5 4 3 2 1

This book is printed on acid-free paper.

Contents

Introduction:
Thinking About
Money

Why Is Money So Important?

"Money makes the world go round."
"Money is the root of all evil."
"Money can't buy you happiness."
"The best things in life are free."

How many of these sayings have you heard? They are just some of the things people say about money. Some of them may seem true, or partly true, to you; some of them may seem wrong. Whatever you think about these sayings, they all tell you one thing: money is very important to people! It's something that they think about—and talk about—a lot.

Why is money so important? On the most basic level, how much money we have determines many other aspects of our lives, such as where we live, what we eat, and how we dress. The amount of money we have may even determine whether we have such essential things as a home, an education, or adequate medical care.

Beyond this basic level, some people feel that the amount of money a person has tells you how important that person is. Sometimes people feel that if they don't have "enough"money—if they can't afford to buy some of the things that they want or that their friends have—there is something "wrong" with them. Sometimes people believe that money is the most important element in their lives, the one element that will make everything else work out right. It's especially easy to believe this if you or your family is having financial problems.

Money isn't just something that affects one person or one family. It has a big impact on the country—and on the world we live in. If a big company moves out of a small town, for example, the entire economy of the town suffers. The people who worked for the company lose their jobs—and so they have much less money to spend. This may mean that local stores receive less money, which may in turn mean that people who work for those stores lose their jobs. At the same time, the company is no longer paying taxes to state and local government. So the government also has less money to spend—and less money for social programs that might help the people who lost their jobs.

In the same way, when the stock market goes up or when a banking chain fails (goes out of business), these events have a big impact on the whole country, sometimes on the whole world. That's why it's important to understand the way money works and the ways it affects the world we live in.

For this reason, there are two parts to this book. Part I, "Money and the Economy," will help you understand money in general. The first chapter in Part I tells you how money was invented, why people use money rather than simply exchanging things, and how the system of money has changed and developed over the years. It also tells you how the United States developed its own system of money. The second chapter in Part I shows you how money affects some major aspects of our country's economy. This chapter explains how banks, the stock market, and government spending may have an impact on your life.

Part II of this book, "Money and You," talks about money in a more personal way. The chapters in this section will help you understand how to get and keep a job; how to make a *budget*, or spending plan; and how to talk to your family about money, whether the issue is a raise in your allowance or the reason your parents think they can't afford to buy you something you want.

How Do You Feel About Money?

Before we go on to look at how money actually works in your life, it may be helpful for you to look at some of your attitudes about money. Here are some statements about money and economic issues. Take a sheet of paper and list the numbers 1 to 10. Next to these numbers mark "yes" or "no" to show which of these statements you agree with:

1. It's more important to have a job you like than one that pays well.
2. The most important thing a parent can give a child is financial security and a good education.
3. I like to put money away for big purchases, like a leather jacket or a stereo, even if it means doing without some other things I want.
4. In general, people in our society put too much emphasis on owning expensive things.
5. I believe that, in general, rich people have worked harder in their lives than poor people and that's why they're so successful.
6. Parents should give their children allowances only when the children have completed their chores.
7. If I had the choice right now, I would take a job that required working several hours a week, so that I could earn more money.
8. People who have lost their jobs should be willing to move to other parts of the country if there are better jobs there.
9. The government has a responsibility to help people in need.

10. Getting into debt is not so bad, as long as you can make the payments on your loans or credit cards.

As you may have guessed, there are no right or wrong opinions on these statements. In fact, every one of these 10 statements is quite controversial. You could probably find several people with widely varying opinions on each statement—just among the people you know.

As you can see, holding different opinions about these questions could lead to vastly different life choices. Do you think a person who disagreed with statement #1 would be likely to follow a career in the arts? Since a career in the arts probably won't pay very well or offer much financial security, someone who values money and security highly would not be likely to make that choice. On the other hand, would a person who agreed with statement #4 be likely to take a boring but well-paying job? Not if he or she is being sincere when saying that people in our society put too much emphasis on owning expensive things.

Because there are so many different attitudes about money in our society, it's important to develop the values about money that are right for you. Money is such an important and controversial issue that many people find themselves in conflict about money issues, with their parents, their dates, or their friends. For example, if two people are dating, what happens if one of them considers money and material things quite important, while the other thinks our society places too much emphasis on those things? You can see how holding these different attitudes might lead to conflicts. If each person believes that his or her attitude is clearly the right one, rather than just one opinion, the conflicts will be even more serious.

Likewise, children and their parents often hold very different views about money. Parents may believe that the greatest satisfaction comes from saving money, while children would rather spend freely today than focus on the future. Or parents may believe that children should "earn" their allowances, while children may feel that they have a right to enough money to allow them to enjoy activities with their friends.

Parent-child conflicts about money are made even more difficult by the fact that usually, the parents are the ones who have the money. That means that, whatever the disagreements, the children are usually the ones who have to give in. But even when children are earning their own money, as with babysitting or part-time jobs, there may be conflicts. A child may be eager to earn extra money by working before or after school, while a parent may feel that studying is more important than earning money. Or parents may feel that if a child wants more money, he or she should earn it, but may restrict the kinds of jobs that the child is allowed to take. Again, these conflicts may be all the more difficult if the two sides don't realize that they have different values—that it's not a matter of one side being "right" and the other side being "wrong."

Different Attitudes About Money

As you can see, people hold many different attitudes about money. Even within the United States, people hold different views depending on their family and cultural backgrounds. And Americans may have vastly different ideas about money than people born in other countries.

Here are some of the factors that can affect people's attitudes toward money:

- whether they have more, less, or the same amount of money as other people in their community
- how closely they live to people who have either a lot less or a lot more money than they do

- how much they hear about people who have either a lot less or a lot more money than they do
- whether their relatives have either a lot less or a lot more money than they do
- their parents' early experiences with money
- whether their parents' current money situation is very different from the one they (their parents) grew up with
- whether their parents' current money situation is very different from the one *their* parents grew up with
- how they—and their family—feel their situation compares with the situations of many people they see on television, in the movies, or in their textbooks
- whether their parents like their jobs
- whether someone in their family is a gambler, a compulsive shopper, or has some other problem with spending
- whether someone in their family is a *hoarder*—a person who goes to extremes in saving things, or who is extremely unwilling to spend money, even on basic necessities like food, clothing, or doctor bills
- whether their community is undergoing a financial crisis such as a plant closing or some other economic problem
- whether their community is affected by racial discrimination, which also relates to poverty and unemployment
- how cutbacks in government spending affect their community

These factors affect people in a variety of ways. Some families react to not having money with shame and embarrassment. Parents in these families might be angry or upset that they can't afford everything they would like to have. They might be especially frustrated that they can't afford to give their children all the toys and treats that their children's friends are used to getting. Of course, if every family in the neighborhood is in the same situation, these parents might be more comfortable with their financial status—or they might still be frustrated and upset, comparing their situations with those of people shown on television or pictured in advertisements.

On the other hand, some parents teach their children not to be ashamed of financial problems—or perhaps even to be a little bit proud of them. Parents in these families might take the attitude that money troubles are an exciting challenge. They might encourage their children to be proud of how well their family pulls together to meet this challenge, and might even encourage them to look down a little bit on other families that "have it soft" or don't have to work so hard to come up with creative ways of handling their financial difficulties.

Sometimes, parents might have one attitude toward money while their children have quite a different attitude. Parents might be proud of their ability to "make do" on very little money, while their children are angry and frustrated that they can't afford the same clothes and toys that their friends have. Or parents might be ashamed of not being able to provide more expensive things for their children, while the children honestly don't care and don't see what the problem is.

People in different cultures have different attitudes about money, too. In some cultures, for example, the family always comes first. If any member of the family is in need, everyone pulls together to help solve the problem—not just parents and children, but also aunts, uncles, cousins, nieces, nephews, grandchildren, and grandparents. In these cultures, family ties are seen as far more important than money.

In other cultures, people are seen as each being financially responsible for themselves. A person might pitch in to help out a relative, but such help is seen as an "extra," not as a basic responsibility. In this type of culture, parents might feel that they have more of an obligation to provide a good life for themselves and their children than to help out more distant relatives.

In some cultures, the most important thing a parent can do is to spend time with the children, even if this means taking a job that pays less well or offers fewer responsibilities. In other cultures, parents are judged more by how good a job they do in providing material things and educations for their children. In these cultures, a parent might be willing to sacrifice time with his or her children in order to provide a higher standard of living for them.

In some cultures, children are seen as the most important members of the family. Parents in these cultures might believe that their first obligation is to make sure that their children have a good education, as well as nice clothing, lots of toys, a nice home to grow up in, and lots of treats and "extras." In other cultures, parents and older relatives are seen as more important than children. In families in these cultures, children might be expected to do without toys or treats in order to provide "extras" for grandparents or elderly aunts and uncles. Children might even be expected to leave school early or to cut short their educations in order to work and bring in money to take care of parents and older relatives.

As you can see, attitudes about money are deeply tied in with the kinds of values people hold. How a person thinks money should be earned and spent will probably tell you a lot about that person's culture, family, and way of life.

Changing Attitudes, Changing Times

Just as people in different cultures have different attitudes about money, so do people brought up in different times view money differently. Attitudes about money in the 1990s are very different from attitudes that were held in the 1930s or 1940s—or even in the 1980s!

At the turn of the century, people's attitudes toward money were far more conservative than they are today. Borrowing and being in debt were viewed as a moral failing, almost as a disgrace. Thrift and saving were highly prized, and people who needed to borrow to make ends meet were seen as careless, flighty, unreliable, or extravagant. The focus in the economy as a whole was on developing large corporations like railroads, oil companies, and other companies that produced basic goods and services.

Then, in the 1920s, the economy changed. A huge network of banks and financial institutions developed, helping money to move more quickly and easily through the economy. At the same time, the economy was increasing its focus on consumer goods—clothing, cars, household appliances, and other things that individuals buy. To help promote the sale of these items, consumers were encouraged to buy *on credit*—that is, to buy goods that they couldn't pay for right away. If they couldn't afford an item, a store or a bank might lend them the money, which they could pay back in *installments*, or parts. That way, people could have goods right away, even if they couldn't afford to pay for them all at once.

With the development of consumer credit and installment purchases, people's attitudes toward debt and spending were undergoing a change. The model citizen was no longer someone who was thrifty, buying only what he or she needed. Instead, advertisements and popular images glorified the person who could fill his or her home with beautiful furniture or labor-saving appliances. People were respected less for being thrifty than for knowing how to use their money to buy as many things as possible.

In the 1930s, the United States, and much of Europe, underwent a profound economic crisis known as the Great Depression. Almost one-third of the American work force was out of work. Many banks failed. This meant that people who had savings accounts or other investments lost all the money they had saved.

In this climate, attitudes toward money changed once again. People who lived through the depression had the experience of seeing great prosperity turn quickly and unexpectedly into enormous poverty. Depression-era citizens—people who are in their sixties and older today—learned through bitter experience that financial security may not last, no matter how thrifty or careful a person has been. They also learned firsthand how painful and upsetting poverty, unemployment, and loss of savings could be. From this experience, a new set of attitudes evolved, one that valued careful planning, restricted spending, and enormous effort put into guaranteeing financial security.

In the United States, the depression was ended in the early 1940s by World War II, which helped revive the American economy. After the war, the economy again focused on consumer spending. Credit in the form of loans and installment plans for consumers once again expanded. Advertisements, movies, and television once again glorified the idea of buying beautiful or appealing objects. Instead of the old ethic of making something last as long as possible, the 1950s saw a value in owning things that were as new and easily replaced as possible. A car or an appliance was not valued because it had lasted a long time with proper care; instead, people valued having the latest model car or the newest washing machine with all the latest gadgets. The term *consumer culture* came into use to describe an economy that was focused on consumers—people who bought things.

In the 1960s, children who had grown up in the consumer culture of the 1950s developed a new set of attitudes about money. They took for granted the prosperity of the 1950s—but rebelled against the importance that decade had put on material things. Many children of the 1960s believed that "the best things in life are free," and that working long hours at dull jobs in order to buy new cars or late-model washing machines was actually a trap. They also found the culture's focus on money and objects wasteful and dangerous to the ecology. During the 1960s and on into the 1970s, popular attitudes changed once again. This time, the value was on doing work for pleasure rather than for money. If necessary, according to the values of the 1960s and the 1970s, people should be willing to buy fewer things or reuse and recycle as many objects as possible in order to avoid the trap of working hard at dull jobs to maintain a high standard of living.

These values in turned changed when the economy went through the severe recessions of the 1970s. Although in the 1960s, many people could find cheap living arrangements and so could afford to live on part-time or volunteer work, by the 1970s, this was far more difficult.

By the 1980s, values had changed again. The gap between the poor and the rich had widened—but for some people, it suddenly seemed far easier to get rich quickly. Some sectors of the economy, particularly law and finance, were rapidly expanding. At the same time, the cost of living was going up. Young people were now much more worried about making money. They also seemed much more excited about the idea of getting a good job and being able to maintain a high standard of living. Whereas in the 1960s and 1970s, people might have been ashamed to admit they wanted to own a fancier stereo or nicer clothes, in the 1980s people were proud to talk about how much money they were earning and how many expensive things they wanted to buy.

At the end of the 1980s, times got harder. As in the 1930s, many people who had thought their prosperity would last forever suddenly found that they had lost their jobs, their investments, and their savings. At the same time, social attitudes changed from a high value on making money and acquiring goods to somewhat greater concern for the poor, the homeless, and those who were not doing well economically.

As you can see, attitudes about money change depending on many factors, including the general economic picture. Of course, the general attitudes that we have described were never held by every single person during a particular time period. Even at the turn of the century, there were people who believed that spending freely was no sin. Even in the 1920s, many people were suspicious of consumer credit and the focus on buying new goods. Even in the 1980s, there were people who were critical of the focus on prosperity when so many were homeless or living in poverty. However, overall attitudes do help shape the context in which you and your family live. They can help make it easier or harder to hold onto certain values, easier or harder to be poor or out of work, easier or harder to hold different values than those of your friends and neighbors or to maintain the values of your own culture.

Coming to Terms with Values About Money

It may be frustrating to realize how many pressures and strains can be associated with the topic of money. Learning about how many factors go into shaping your and your family's ideas may at first seem overwhelming, as though the forces affecting your and your family's thinking are large, powerful, and beyond your control.

However, the more aware you are of all the different factors that affect your thinking about money, the more free you are to choose your own values and make your own decisions about this all-important area of life. Realizing what your ideas are and where they come from can help you clarify where you agree and where you disagree with your friends, your family, and the society as a whole. This awareness of your own values and your own feelings can help you make more satisfying decisions about how to handle money, how to choose the kind of work you want, and how to respond to all the political and social issues that involve money and the economy.

This book is your resource. Use it to learn more about how money works and how the economy functions. Use it also to learn more about how you and the people in your life feel and think about money and to help you think further about your attitudes. The more clearly you think about this issue, the more control and satisfaction you will have in dealing with money and with its influence in your life.

Part I

MONEY AND THE ECONOMY

1

A History of Money

Money is something we take for granted in our lives. It's hard to imagine how we would get food, clothing, shelter, and all the other things we need without paying for them with money. But actually, money had to be invented. For most of the thousands of years people have been living on the earth, there was no money.

Exchange, Barter, and Trade

Before people invented money, they used to exchange or *barter* goods. To barter something is to trade it for something else of equal value. Within a community, a person whose hen laid extra eggs might barter them for some milk or leather from a person with an extra cow. People who lived near a forest might barter wood for salt or fish from people who lived by the ocean.

Can you picture how this early system of barter must have worked? Without money, people had to figure out each exchange from the beginning, each time. Even if two neighbors figured out how many eggs they wanted to trade for a quantity of milk, they still wouldn't know how much milk to trade for a load of wood or a bushel of corn. Every exchange would take place on its own terms, with no way to measure one exchange against another.

This kind of piece-by-piece exchange worked in very simple economies, but once trade became more complicated, the barter system became cumbersome and difficult to use. As long as people were primarily growing food or raising animals for their own use and trading only the little bit that was left over, it didn't matter that trade might be difficult and complicated because it was only a very small part of the economy anyway. But when people began making trade a bigger part of their lives, and particularly when traders began traveling around the world, carrying goods from one part of the globe to another, they needed a better system of exchange. Traders needed a way to measure and compare the values of different goods, so that they could tell how to exchange many different types of goods for one another.

For example, if you were a trader traveling between the Spice Islands in the Far East and the lands of Europe further west, you might be carrying cinnamon, pepper, and other spices from the East to trade for the furs and amber (a kind of precious stone) of Europe. In order to know how to make the most profitable exchange, you would have to be able to compare the value of each spice, so that you'd know which of the spices was most valuable. Likewise, you'd have to know the different values of different types of fur and how to compare the price of fur and the price of amber. Only by being able to compare different values could you make intelligent business decisions about which goods to trade; you could then spend more time and energy on the goods that were more valuable, and less time and energy on goods that were less valuable.

Traders also needed a way to exchange goods that didn't depend on literally trading one item for another. Direct exchange worked well enough when two traders lived near each other or could visit each other easily. But what about trade that extended all through the great landmasses of Europe and Asia, or that passed across the oceans between Europe, China, and India? In fact, few traders made this entire trip by themselves. Instead, each trader traveled only a short way along the route, passing the goods on to another trader to take further. They needed some way to exchange and pass goods along without literally carrying the items to be exchanged all the way along the trade route.

For example, a trader might carry furs from Europe along a trade route until he reached a seaport. There he might sell his goods to a sea trader, who would take European furs across the Red Sea into the Middle East. On the other side of the Red Sea, this second trader might sell his goods to a third trader, who would go further into Asia, sell the European furs, and buy Far Eastern spices. But this third trader might not carry the spices back to Europe himself. Instead, he would sell them to a fourth trader, who in turn would travel back across the Red Sea to Europe, where he would sell the spices to a fifth trader, and so on.

As you can see, these more complicated trade relations required a more complicated system than direct barter. In order to buy and sell goods along a lengthy trade route, some kind of standard medium of exchange was needed. *Money* was a unit that could be exchanged at all times and all places for a whole variety of goods. Instead of directly trading eggs for milk, or furs for spices, a trader could *buy* eggs by trading money for them, or *sell* milk by giving it away in exchange for money.

Thus, money did two things:

1. Money was a standard unit that could be exchanged for a whole variety of things. That made it easier for people to compare the values of different goods in order to make intelligent business decisions about what to trade.
2. Money was a standard unit that could be exchanged in many different places. That meant that goods could be moved along a trade route by many different traders, who kept exchanging different goods for money all along the route.

Early Forms of Money

In addition, money had a third advantage: it could be small and easy to carry, which made it convenient for trading against a whole range of huge items. Of course, the earliest forms of money were far different from the coins and bills we use for money today. Today's money can *only* be used as a form of exchange. You don't use dollar bills as wallpaper, or copper pennies to help conduct electricity in batteries. You *could* use paper and metal money in this way—but you don't, because the money can be exchanged for goods that are worth more than the paper or metal it is made out of.

By contrast, the first forms of money, used over 5,000 years ago, were small, valuable items that could be used *both* as exchange *and* for their own value. People used a wide range of items as money: seeds, rocks, leather, furs, cows, sheep, tobacco, beads, shells, rocks, and fish-hooks. People also traded many items that could not be used for anything except exchange: dogs' teeth, birds' feathers, the bristles from an elephant's tail, even dead rats. In Mongolia, people used tea as money. Many peoples, including the Ethiopians, the ancient Romans, and the

Chinese, used salt, which in those days was rare and valuable since it could be used to preserve meat, fish, and other foods before the days of refrigerators and preservatives. In fact, the current English word *salary*—the money that an employee receives—comes from the Roman word for *salt*.

As people around the world experimented with different types of money, they came up with some very creative solutions. The ancient Greeks used *obelas*—units of money that were smaller than the seed of an apple. Obelas were so small, people used to carry them in their mouths. The people on the Pacific island of Santa Cruz used feathers to exchange as money. On the other hand, the Pacific islanders on Yap used money stones that were more than 12 feet tall, weighing more than 500 pounds!

Can you see a problem with these early forms of money? Some of them could fall apart, get lost, or get broken very easily. Others, like sheep, cows, and the Yap people's stones, were pretty hard to carry around for quick trading! So finally, about 5,000 years ago in a part of the ancient world known as Mesopotamia (the territory occupied by present-day Iraq), people began using metal for money. Metal money was light and durable. It could be stamped with an impression that gave it different values, the way our quarters are stamped with the words *quarter dollar* and our pennies with the words *one cent*. Eventually, metal money caught on.

People used all sorts of metal for the first money, including gold, silver, bronze, copper, iron, lead, and tin. At first, people simply used the metal itself for money, the way they had used salt, tea, feathers, or shells. Then they got the idea of using *coins*—pieces of metal stamped with information about how much each piece could be exchanged for. The metal itself might not be worth very much, but the information printed on the metal told people that they could use each coin to stand for greater values. (In the same way, the value of the metal in a quarter or a nickel wouldn't be worth twenty-five or five cents if you melted those coins down—

but the information on each coin tells you how much it can be exchanged for.)

Although we know that the people of Mesopotamia used metal for money about 5,000 years ago, we aren't sure whether they used actual coins. The Mesopotamians might just have exchanged bits of metal. Some scholars speculate that the people of Egypt may have been the first to use coins, sometime around 2500 B.C. All scholars agree, however, that the first clearly recorded use of marked coins was by the Greeks, just after 700 B.C. By that time, each Greek city had its own coins.

Both the Greeks and the Romans *minted*, or made coins. Today we also use the word *mint* to mean the place where coins are made and stored. The Romans called that place by the Latin word *moneta*—the ancestor of the English word *money.*

The Development of Money

Even after coins were developed, the world was still a long way away from our current system of money. For one thing, each city made its own coins, with no agreed-upon way of exchanging one type of coin for another. If you were a trader from Athens, how would you know how much your Athenian coins would buy in the city of Rome? Gradually, traders worked out different *rates of exchange*—ways of exchanging one type of money for another. But this was a long, slow process that was often worked out differently depending on the individual trader.

Another complication lay in the fact that for thousands of years, most people did not use money for most important purchases. Rich people might use money to trade, to pay taxes, or for other major transactions, but ordinary people continued to exchange and barter for most things in their daily lives. A worker, for example, would be paid in food, clothing, and shelter, rather than in money. A farming family would grow food and make items for themselves, trading the tiny surplus for whatever they could not make or grow themselves.

Eventually, as trade and exchange became ever more important parts of the world economy, people began to use paper money as well as coins. Paper money had a lot of advantages: it was lighter and easier to carry, and it was also a lot cheaper to make. The use of paper money meant that people had really grasped the difference between money as a symbol—the things you can exchange money to buy—and money as an actual thing—the actual cost of the paper and ink in a dollar bill or other type of paper money.

The first use of paper money that we know about was in China, in around A.D. 1300. The first use of paper money in Europe took place in Sweden, in the 1600s. The 1600s were a time of extensive international trade and exploration. Paper money made trade easier and more efficient, so its use quickly caught on throughout Europe.

Money in the United States

At the time the first European colonies were being established in America, European countries were still primarily using coins. British, Spanish, and French coins were used in the new American colonies, reflecting the European countries that had sent traders, soldiers, and settlers to North America.

In 1652, Massachusetts issued the first American coins, which were known as shillings (worth about 12 cents each), sixpences (worth six "pennies" or "pence"), and threepences. These coins were in the same *denominations*, or amounts, as British money, reflecting the fact that

Massachusetts had been settled by people from Britain. Later, other colonies issued their own coins. In 1690, the Massachusetts Bay Colony also established a bank and issued paper money, which was primarily used for paying soldiers.

However, as in Europe, most people in America did not depend on money. Instead, they relied a great deal on barter. Gunpowder and bullets were frequently bartered, since everybody needed these items for hunting and self-defense.

Another type of bartering involved human beings. Many people wanted to come to America during colonial times but couldn't afford the price of the ocean voyage. They bartered themselves, offering to work for seven years for any person who would pay their fare and give them room and board in the new country when they came over. These workers were called *indentured servants.*

When the 13 colonies rebelled against Great Britain and became the United States, the new nation needed to have its own money. The Continental Congress issued paper money to pay soldiers' salaries and other expenses of the new government. These notes were called *Continentals.*

During the American Revolution, the Congress kept printing more and more Continentals to keep up with the new expenses of the government. At the same time, crucial goods like food, clothing, guns and gunpowder became more and more scarce. As a result, the value of each Continental—the amount of goods that it could be exchanged for—kept going down. Another way of explaining this is to say that prices went up. The same amount of cheese that could be bought for one or two Continentals when the war started cost more than a whole barrel of Continentals by the time the war ended. This process—prices going up, so that it costs more money to buy the same thing—is known as *inflation.*

Inflation takes place when the amount of money in circulation does not match the amount of wealth that a society has. Simply printing more money does not mean there are more goods to buy or more people to work longer hours. Instead, it simply means that it takes more money to buy the same things.

Inflation happens more easily with paper money than with coins because it is so cheap and easy to print paper money. That's what happened during the American Revolution. Many more Continentals were printed, but new wealth—goods and services—was not being produced. In fact, the war was using up many goods, so that for civilians, there was a shortage. (This often happens during wartime, or during a time when a country's military budget is very large.) Even though there were fewer products to buy, there was more money—so each product ended up costing more. Perhaps if the government had been using only coins, instead of paper money, it would not have found it so easy to manufacture so much money, and inflation would have been slowed or prevented.

At any rate, that's what the people running the American economy believed at the time. The United States had had such a difficult time with Continentals that it stopped using paper money altogether for many years—until Civil War times in the 1860s. Instead, in 1792, the United States began to mint its own new coins in the first U.S. mint, in Philadelphia.

Although the United States was not using paper money, it had established the dollar—one hundred cents—as its unit of money in 1785. Until that year, foreign money was used freely in the United States. After 1785, however, the new country had its own type of money.

Despite the new system of coining money, however, bartering continued in the new United States, and many different items of value were used as a kind of money. For example, the governor of the state of Tennessee was paid a "salary" of 200 deerskins a year. One of the governor's clerks was paid in beaver skins, which were considered less valuable. The governor and his clerk could trade these skins for other items that they needed more.

Paper Money in the United States

Although for many years paper money wasn't used by ordinary people in the United States, banks printed *bank notes* as records of large amounts of money. These bank notes were used by rich people and big traders to represent the exchange of huge sums. The note was a kind of promise by the bank that it would exchange the piece of paper for gold or silver worth the amount printed on the paper. However, sometimes banks would issue more notes than they had gold and silver to back them up. A person trying to exchange his or her bank notes would discover that he or she had lost everything.

To correct this situation, the government decided that it should regulate the distribution of money. In 1862, the first U.S. paper dollar was authorized—green bills known as "greenbacks." However, even though the government was now issuing greenbacks, banks were still printing their own bank notes. Different banks put out different types of money, which led to great confusion. No one could be sure how much each different bill or bank note was really worth. Also, some bills were *counterfeit*—printed falsely, with no government wealth to back them up. U.S. government wealth was traditionally based on how much gold was held in federal banks.

Finally, in 1913, the U.S. Treasury Department took over all printing and issuing of money. This establishment of a standard *currency*, or form of money, meant that everyone could be sure of exactly what every piece of money was worth. The bills used in 1913 were bigger than the money we use today. In 1929, U.S. money was redesigned. In that year, the United States started using money of the size and design that we use today.

How Money Is Made

In order to prevent the printing of counterfeit money, the United States government prints paper money at one place only: the Bureau of Engraving and Printing in Washington,

D.C. *Engraving* is the process of carving a design into soft steel. The designs that we use on our money are carefully engraved, with the help of a magnifying glass, so that engravers can make sure that every tiny line is in the right place. That way, a counterfeiter will have a much harder time making a copy of a bill—the design includes so many small, intricate lines that it is almost impossible to copy.

Once a steel engraving of a new design is made, the steel plate is covered with ink. This ink-covered engraving can be used to stamp ink onto hundreds of pieces of paper—which get cut up into money. The paper used is a special secret blend of linen and cotton with small amounts of colored fibers blended in. The blend is secret so that counterfeiters will not be able to duplicate it. The ink used to make money is also a secret blend. It is illegal for anyone to make this type of paper or ink without special permission from the Bureau of Engraving and Printing.

The money-printing process occurs in two stages. First, the bill's face is printed with black ink. This ink must be allowed to dry. Then the back of the bill is also printed with black ink. This, too, must dry. Finally the bill is printed again with green ink.

Bills are printed in large sheets, with 32 bills per sheet. When all the ink is completely dry, the big sheets are cut into 32 pieces.

A dollar bill's average life span is only 17 to 18 months. After that, a piece of money is usually old, worn, and ragged. Banks send this worn-out money to the Federal Reserve Bank, a national bank whose duties include controlling the supply of money in the country. At the Federal Reserve, the money is shredded into tiny pieces no wider than one-sixteenth of an inch. Then the pieces are burned and new money is printed to take the place of the old money.

Sometimes odd things happen to money that cause it to wear out sooner than usual. Money may get caught in a fire, chewed by a cow, or soaked and ripped in a rainstorm. (Once a person hid some money in a shotgun and forgot about it—until the gun was fired!) All of this damaged money has to be burnt by the Federal Reserve and replaced by the U.S. Treasury.

Coins also have a special process of manufacture. Currently, coins are made of copper and nickel. At one time, the government made coins out of gold and silver because these metals were more valuable. Unlike paper money, coins were more likely to be worth something in themselves because metal was more expensive than paper. Finally, however, the government shifted to using coins made out of cheaper materials. Like paper money, coins are now valuable not because they are made from expensive ingredients but because they represent wealth that exists somewhere else.

Dimes and quarters are made with *milled* edges—edges with tiny ridges. That's because in the old days, when coins were made from gold and silver, some people used to shave the edges off the coins, melt them down, and sell the extra precious metals. Milled edges meant that no one could trim the coins in this way.

Today, coins are made of metal melted in an electric furnace. The *molten* (melted) metal is poured into steel molds, known as *ingots,* and allowed to cool. The ingots are then rolled out like cookie dough into long flat sheets that are just as thick as the coins that will be made. Blank disks the size of coins are punched out of the sheets of metal, just the way a cookie-cutter punches cookies out of a sheet of dough.

After the disks are punched out, they are heated up again. Special acids are used to clean and polish them, eating away any dirt, bumps, or ridges. These new, clean pieces of metal then go into an "upsetting" machine that presses out raised rims around the edges, which makes the coins more difficult to counterfeit.

Once the coins have left the upsetting machine, they go down a tube into a press where their heads and tails are imprinted with the correct design. If any coins come through this procedure with mistakes, they are melted and the process starts all over again.

How to "Read" a Bill and a Coin

You've probably noticed that money is covered with many different symbols—pictures, numbers, and letters. Have you ever wondered what they all mean? Each symbol on a piece of money has a meaning of its own.

Look at the face of a one-dollar bill, the side with the picture of George Washington on it. The signature in the lower left-hand corner is that of the person who is treasurer of the United States at the time the bill is printed, while the signature in the lower right-hand corner is that of the secretary of the Treasury.

The green number in both the lower left and the upper right corners is called the *serial number*. Every single bill printed in the United States has its own serial number. That way, every bill can be identified. Counterfeiters who make several bills with the same number can be more easily caught. Money used for illegal purposes, such as arms trading or drug dealing, can often be traced and identified through serial numbers.

To the left of George Washington's picture is a large letter surrounded by the words *Federal Reserve Bank* and the name of a city. The letter is also a code, naming which Federal Reserve Bank branch has issued this particular piece of money. Here is the code used on dollar bills:

A — Boston
B — New York
C — Philadelphia
D — Cleveland
E — Richmond
F — Atlanta
G — Chicago
H — St. Louis
I — Minneapolis
J — Kansas City
K — Dallas
L — San Francisco

Just to the right of the picture of George Washington, between the picture and the signature of the secretary of the Treasury, is a little notation that reads "Series" and a date. This shows the date that the bill's design was first used. A bill's design changes every time there is a new treasurer or secretary of the Treasury.

In green ink, superimposed on the word *ONE* is a circle marked *The Department of the Treasury.* This is the official seal of the Treasury Department. The seal includes the year 1789, the date the department was founded, as well as the symbols of a pair of scales—symbolizing justice—and a key, symbolizing the key that the department uses to lock up the country's money. You can also see 13 little stars on the seal, standing for the original 13 states.

There are more symbols on the other side of the bill. The two circles on the bill's back are the two sides of the Great Seal of the United States. This seal is marked with three mottoes in Latin. *Annuit Coeptis* means "He [God] has favored our undertaking." *Novus Ordo Seclorum* means "A new secular [nonreligious] order." *E Pluribus Unum* means "Out of many, one," referring to the process of forming one nation out of many colonies or states.

The pyramid on the left side of the bill has 13 layers of brick, representing the 13 original colonies. The unfinished space between the bricks and the eye means that there is still more room for the nation to grow. The eye at the top of the pyramid is the eye of God, watching over the United States. If you look closely, you can see the Roman numerals for 1776 at the base of the pyramid, representing the year of the Declaration of Independence.

The eagle on the right side of the seal is clutching an olive branch for peace in one claw and a bunch of arrows for war in the other. This means that the eagle—symbol of the United States—is ready for either peace or war. However, the eagle's head is turned toward the olive branch, meaning that the United States will always prefer peace if given the choice. The olive branch has 13 leaves and there are 13 arrows, referring again to the original 13 colonies. There are also 13 stars in the cloud over the eagle's head.

A coin also has many symbols on it. If you look at a quarter, for example, you'll see a tiny letter just to the right of the face. The letter tells you where the coin was minted, according to the following code:

D — Denver
O — New Orleans
P — Philadelphia
S — San Francisco

Great American leaders are honored by having their pictures put on bills and coins. Here is a list telling you which leader is on which piece of money:

One-dollar bill—George Washington
Two-dollar bill—Thomas Jefferson
Five-dollar bill—Abraham Lincoln
Ten-dollar bill—Alexander Hamilton
Twenty-dollar bill—Andrew Jackson
Fifty-dollar bill—Ulysses S. Grant
Hundred-dollar bill—Benjamin Franklin
Penny—Abraham Lincoln
Nickel—Thomas Jefferson
Dime—Franklin D. Roosevelt
Quarter—George Washington
Fifty-cent piece—John F. Kennedy
Silver dollar—Susan B. Anthony

Only three of these leaders were not presidents. Alexander Hamilton was the first secretary of the Treasury, under President George Washington. Benjamin Franklin was a founder of the United States who helped inspire the ideals of the revolutionary war and was one of the people who wrote the U.S. Constitution. Susan B. Anthony was a pioneer in the fight for women's rights, especially the right to vote.

Money in Circulation Today

Today, the highest bill in circulation is the one-hundred-dollar bill. The Bureau of Engraving and Printing used to make bills of $500, $1,000, $5,000, $10,000, and $100,000 amounts, for payments between banks and other large traders. Once checks, credit cards, and other forms of exchange came into fashion, however, these large bills were no longer used.

Today there is approximately $215 billion worth of money circulating in the United States in coins and bills. Of course, a great deal more wealth is represented in bank deposits, stock holdings, credit lines, and other forms of exchange. In the next chapter, we'll look at some of the new ways of representing money, and at how money and the economy may be affecting your family and your community.

2

The Economy: Wages and Prices, Banks, the Stock Market, and the Government

---

The economy can seem like a complicated and over-whelming subject. Yet the United States economy affects everyone who lives in this country—as well as many other people around the world—so it is worth our while to try to understand how it works and specifically how it affects us.

What Is "The Economy"?

The *economy* is the system by which goods and services are distributed among the people in a society. *Economics* is the study of the economic system. An *economist* is someone who studies the economy.

One of the reasons the economy is so hard to understand is that even economists—experts who spend their lives studying this topic—disagree deeply about it. There are many different theories about how and why the economy works the way it does.

Economists study—and disagree about—a wide variety of topics. Some of these topics are very specific, such as how wages and prices are set and whether they are likely to go up or down; what the level of employment and unemployment is, and what it is likely to be in the future; what the *standard of living*—the level of comfort and prosperity—of most people will be, and whether it will go up or down.

Economists also study bigger questions as they look at the entire economic system of a country. For example, they might look at what type of products a country is likely to manufacture. Will it specialize in heavy *industrial* goods used in industries and factories; in *consumer* goods used by individuals, such as automobiles and washing machines; in *agricultural products*, such as processed coffee beans and cotton; or in some mixture of all of these goods?

Some countries in the world today, such as Saudi Arabia, specialize in one product, such as oil. Other countries, such as Japan, have become major exporters of electronic products. As you can imagine, the types of goods a country specializes in will have important consequences for the amount of wealth there is in that country. If a country does not make enough of a certain product on its own, it will have to *import*, or bring in, that product from somewhere else. This means that the country has less money to spend on other things, since a portion of its wealth is going to pay for something manufactured elsewhere. Thus, if Saudi Arabia must import automobiles, for example, or if Japan must import food, this has serious consequences for their economies. Some economists study what these consequences are and make suggestions for how a country can handle the situation.

A related topic that economists study is how an economy changes over the years. If a country has primarily produced coffee or cotton while importing manufactured goods, for example, it might want to try to develop the manufacturing sector of its economy. If a country has specialized in old-fashioned heavy industrial goods, it might need to switch over to more modern electronic products. Economists look at how these changes can be made and at what effect they have on the people of a country.

Finally, an important topic in the study of economics has to do with how various countries compete and interact in the world market. The United States, for example, has been a world leader in many manufacturing sectors for many years. Now, however, Germany is a key competitor in industrial goods, while Japan is a competitor in electronics. This type of competition has important consequences for the economy of the United States and thus for the lives of all its citizens.

Sometimes it's difficult to grasp why economics is an important topic or what difference it makes to us. Here are just some of the ways economic questions affect us in our daily lives. They affect

- whether you and the people in your family will be able to find work
- what type of work you'll be able to find
- how well the work you find will pay
- whether you'll need frequent raises just to break even, or whether you'll be able to keep improving your standard of living
- whether the goods that you can buy in a store are of high or low quality
- whether you and the people in your family feel confident that you'll be able to find work, or whether you feel scared and threatened, willing to do anything in order to keep a job
- whether you and your family will be able to stay in the area you're now living in, or whether plant closings and other changes in the economy will mean that jobs will only be available somewhere else

- whether neighborhood stores stay in business or go out of business
- whether schools, libraries, and other public services in your community have enough money to operate or are undergoing funding shortages
- whether police, firefighters, and other public employees in your community have enough money to serve you and your neighbors, or whether they are undergoing funding shortages
- whether you can afford the kind of education that you want
- whether high-quality public community colleges, colleges, and universities are available to you, and how much tuition they charge

Can you think of other ways in which the economy affects you, your family, and your community?

As we have seen, the economy doesn't just affect money. It has an impact on a great many aspects of people's lives, including many key political and social issues. In turn, political and social issues affect the economy.

The question of equal pay for equal work, for example, is both an economic and a political question. Whether people should receive the same pay for the same work, or whether it's all right to pay differently based on race, gender, sexual preference, handicap, or some other factor that doesn't affect the actual work being done, is an issue of hot debate. Some employers will claim—or have claimed in the past—that they can't afford to give equal pay for equal work, or that such a policy makes it harder to get certain people to do a job. Some workers might claim that equal pay for equal work is the only fair policy, whether the employer can afford it or not. Some economists have said that equal pay for equal work is good for the economy; others have argued that it is detrimental.

Pollution is another problem that has both a political and an economic side. Government agencies may pass laws to regulate pollution—but corporate heads may argue that they cannot afford to obey these laws. Consumers may believe that these laws result in higher prices; workers may believe that they result in loss of jobs. On the other hand, consumers, workers, and some economists might argue that corporations can easily afford to obey antipollution laws; they will simply have to be satisfied with lower profits. Still others might say that antipollution laws may be costly, but they are important just the same.

Over the years, there have been many arguments and political fights in the United States over issues that are both economic and political. What rights a worker has on the job, for example, is a hotly contested issue. Some people believe that workers should have the right to form *unions*—organizations to protect themselves and their rights and to push for higher pay. Other people believe that unions are unfair, since they limit the freedom of employers to run businesses in their own way.

Likewise, the question of whether people have the right to get paid for overtime, to be free of sexual harassment (in which a worker is subjected to unwanted sexual advances or sexual comments), or to say no to dangerous or degrading work, is both an economic and a political question. In an economy where jobs are scarce, workers may be more nervous about fighting for their rights. Or they may feel so desperate that they are *more* willing to fight. On the other hand, in a booming economy, workers may feel that they are earning so much money that these other rights matter less to them. Or they may feel more confident and secure about making demands. Either way, political and economic issues interact.

The questions of how many hours a day people work, how many hours a week they work, what type of medical and retirement benefits they receive, and how quickly or slowly their salaries increase over the years are also political and economic questions. Sometimes these issues are decided by the economy alone—by the decisions of business owners. Sometimes, however, government regulations, pressures from unions, or a general climate of public opinion influences or even enforces certain decisions.

Finally, the question of what welfare benefits, medical help, unemployment insurance, and other benefits people receive when they are out of work is both a political and an economic issue. If tax money is tight, it is more difficult to find the money for these benefits. On the other hand, if there is a great deal of political pressure to fund these areas, then perhaps the money can come from some other part of the economy.

As you can see, economic issues play an extremely important role in the lives of you, your family, and your neighbors. In this chapter, we'll cover some of the basic facts about our economy, facts on which most economists can agree. We'll also describe three key economic institutions—banks, the stock market, and the government.

Capitalist Economy

The United States has what is known as a *capitalist* economy. The word *capital* means the industrial goods—the machines and the tools—that are used to make products and produce wealth. In a capitalist economy, the capital is owned privately. That is, individual people or groups of people—called *corporations*—own all the factories, tools, machines, computers, raw materials, and all the other physical things that produce wealth. People who don't own capital must go to work as employees of the people who do own capital.

There are many other types of economies. In the world today, the other major type of economy is known as a *socialist* economy. It gets its name from the principle that wealth is owned *socially*, by the society as a whole rather than by individuals. There are many different types of socialism in the world today, but all socialist economies follow the principle that, for the most part, the most important industries cannot be owned by single individuals or groups of individuals. Instead, they are supposed to be owned by society as a whole.

Socialist economies are generally *planned* economies. That is, the government in some way decides on *prices*—what things will cost—and on *wages*—how much money workers will receive. In a capitalist economy, each company is free to set its own prices and wages. However, generally, prices and wages fall within certain ranges. One company might charge $10,000 for its compact economy car, whereas another company might charge $11,000, and another company $9,500. But it would be very unusual to find one company charging only $1,000 for a compact car, while another company charged $100,000. Although companies are free to set their own prices, certain principles come into play that help determine how it happens that prices tend to cluster within a fairly small range.

Likewise, although each company is free to set its own wages, there is a certain range that wages tend to fall into. Nurses, for example, might make $10.00 an hour at Hospital A and only $9.50 at Hospital B. However, it would be very unlikely for one hospital to pay nurses only $4.50 an hour, and another hospital to pay them as much as $100 an hour. Although each hospital is basically free to set its own wages, certain principles come into play here, too.

There are many different theories to explain how wages and prices fall into the patterns that they do. The most widespread is called the *law of supply and demand*. This "law" is very simple. It states that if something is scarce—if *supply* is low—people will pay more for it. If something is common—if *supply* is high—people won't want to pay very much for it. If people are willing to pay a lot for a good or a service—if *demand* is high—its price or wage will go up. If people are not willing to pay very much—if *demand* is low—its price or wage will go down.

At the same time, if people can get the same thing for less money, they will almost certainly choose to buy the cheaper product. Thus if people believe that two cars are equally good, they are much more likely to buy the car that costs $9,500 than the car that costs $10,000 or $11,000. Every car company is then caught between two forces. On the one hand, it wants to charge as much as it can, so it will make as much money as possible. On the other hand, it wants to charge as little money as it can, so it will beat out the other car companies and sell more cars. If it charges too much, its cars will be too expensive and no one will buy them. If it charges too little, it may sell a lot of cars, but it won't make very much money. So prices get set as each company tries to steer its way between these two forces.

Wages work the same way. On the one hand, employers want to pay employees as little as possible in order to make more money. On the other hand, employees want to earn as much money as possible. So employees will choose the employers who pay the most, while employers will choose the employees that they can pay the least. If there is a shortage of nurses, employers will be competing with each other, each trying to pay nurses more so that more nurses will come to work for them. In that case, wages will go up. If there are a lot of nurses, the nurses will be competing with each other, each willing to take less money in order to get one of the scarce jobs. In that case, wages will probably go down.

Here, too, there are certain limits on the whole process. A nurse can't take less than a certain amount, because he or she won't be able to survive on too small a salary. If nursing salaries get too low, nurses will just stop taking nursing jobs altogether and will go into some other line of work. On the other hand, hospitals can't pay more than a certain amount, or they might not have any money left over for other things. If nursing salaries get too high, hospitals might make do with fewer nurses or simply go out of business.

What we've just described is the simplest version of the law of supply and demand. This is how the process works *in theory*. In practice, however, the economy is much more complicated. Many different factors affect how wages and prices are set, along with the ones we've mentioned. Here are some other factors that affect prices:

- **advertising**—People may want an expensive product because they believe it will make them sexy, smart, or successful, and they may be willing to pay extra as a result.
- **prestige**—People may be willing to spend more than they can afford for certain products that they think will make other people admire or envy them.
- **size of company**—If the biggest companies in a field all set their prices high, consumers won't have any choice. If oil prices are high, for example, anybody who wants to drive a car will have to pay a high price for gasoline at every single gas station. If all the big oil companies agree to set their prices high, a little oil company that can't afford to advertise and only has one service station will probably go out of business, even if its gas is half the price of the big companies' gas.

Can you think of other factors that might affect an item's price?

Here are some of the factors that might affect wages:

- **discrimination**—Historically, women have earned less than men, and people of color have earned less than white people. Discrimination against homosexuals, the handicapped, and immigrants are also frequently practiced. If people are scared, beaten down, or treated badly in other ways, they may accept lower wages even if their jobs are necessary and important.
- **unions**—A *union* is a group of employees organized to improve wages and working conditions. A union's biggest weapon is the *strike*—when all employees stop working until they get what they want. Companies are often afraid that strikes will cost them money or hurt their

business in some other way. If all the employees at a company stick together, they may be able to affect the wages that a company pays them.

- **prestige and pleasure**—Some jobs are considered more prestigious or enjoyable, and so people may be willing to accept less money for doing them. Many jobs in the arts, for example, pay very low wages because there is high prestige associated with them and because many people want to work in the arts. On the other hand, some jobs are considered dangerous, degrading, or dull, and people may require more money for doing them.

Can you think of other factors that would affect how wages are set?

Inflation, Recession, and Depression

One of the major problems in our economy is inflation. Inflation is a situation in which prices are going up faster than wages. Thus a person has to work more hours to pay for the same items.

For example, let's say that this year a loaf of bread costs $1.00 and the average salary in the United States is $10.00 per hour. That means that a person could earn enough money to buy a loaf of bread in one-tenth of an hour, or six minutes.

Then, halfway through the year, the price of bread goes up to $1.25, while wages stay the same. That means that a person now has to work one-eighth of an hour—seven and a half minutes—to buy the same loaf of bread.

Now let's say that at the end of the year, wages go up to $11.00 per hour, but the price of bread goes up to $1.50. Now a person has to work more than one-seventh of an hour—over eight minutes—to buy the same loaf of bread.

As you can see, if more and more work time is spent earning money to buy loaves of bread, that leaves employees a lot less money left over to buy other things. Inflation means that the same money buys fewer things—and everybody's standard of living goes down, even if salaries are going up.

As with most economic issues, economists disagree deeply about exactly what causes inflation. They generally do agree that a sharp increase in the cost of one essential item is likely to be a contributing factor. When oil prices rose sharply in the mid-1970s, inflation went up sharply. That's because all the companies that used oil—to heat their buildings or run their machines—suddenly had to raise their prices to cover the increased cost of the oil. At the same time, all the consumers who bought oil or oil products—mainly in the form of gasoline for their cars—had to spend a much bigger portion of their paychecks on oil. All of a sudden, consumers were hit with higher prices for oil and for many other things. These higher prices were a form of inflation.

Because they were hurt by this sudden increase in oil prices, many companies went out of business or cut back on their growth. They fired or laid off people, or stopped hiring. They also lowered wages whenever they could. As a result, people who were now unemployed or working for lower wages could not afford to buy as many things as they had before. As they bought less, companies sold less. That meant that *more* companies fell on hard times—laying off more workers and cutting back more on wages. This vicious cycle of hard times is known as a *recession.*

A recession is a period of economic difficulty that is severe but not as severe as a *depression. Depression* is the word used to describe the most severe type of difficulty in an economy. During the Great Depression that began in 1929, for example, almost one-third of the United States work force was out of work. Hundreds of thousands of people were suddenly poor. Many were thrown out of their apartments because they could not pay their rent, or they had their homes taken away when they could not pay their mortgages. Farmers lost their farms, small business owners lost their businesses, and many big business owners had trouble selling their products and keeping their companies going.

Another topic on which economists disagree is how to stop a recession or a depression. Many people believe that President Ronald Reagan was successful in stopping the recession of the 1970s by cutting taxes on corporations, removing other restrictions on businesses, increasing military spending, and cutting back on government social programs. Other people believe that, although some people benefited from Reagan's activities, many other people fell into severe poverty as a result. Furthermore, critics charge, the prosperity that Reagan created lasted only a short time, and was followed by more severe economic problems. These debates seem likely to continue throughout the 1990s.

Banks in Our Time

One very important institution in our economy is the bank. A bank's job is to manage money for people, corporations, and the government. Both individuals and corporations can store their money in banks.

Banks provide a number of important services to you and your family as well as to corporations. First and foremost, they are a safe place to store your money. They also provide a way to transfer money from one place to another, by writing a check. A check is a piece of paper that authorizes the bank to give your money to the person or business whose name is on the check.

Banks also lend money to corporations and to people. Individuals use bank loans to buy or repair a home, pay for a college education, to expand or start a business, or to meet personal financial obligations. When people or corporations borrow money from a bank, they must pay *interest*—a percentage of the money borrowed.

Although banks do provide services to individuals, that is not their main function. A bank's main function is to lend large sums of money. Banks get their money from individuals and corporations. They pay interest on the money that they hold, and charge interest on the money that they lend.

In order to make a profit, they must collect more interest than they pay out.

Sometimes, too, banks *invest* money as well as lend it. To invest money means to put it into a corporation or into some business project such as opening a mine, building a housing complex, or doing medical research. All of these projects cost money, which comes from investors. If the project makes money, the investors get back some of the profits, again in the form of a percentage of the money they paid out. Most businesses need loans and investments at various times, and banks are an important source of both.

The History of Banking

Banks have a very interesting history. In ancient times, thousands of years ago, people kept their valuables in temples because they believed that the gods would punish anyone who robbed from a temple. Because so many valuables were kept in temples, people who worked in temples began making loans. If someone had left a pile of gold and silver in the temple, rather than let the gold and silver sit there, the temple worker might loan it out to someone who needed it. As long as the person repaid the loan before the real owner asked for the metals back, there would be no problem.

Archaeologists have found records over 2,000 years old showing the amount of precious metal that people deposited in a temple in Babylon (in today's country of Iraq), as well as records showing when and how people borrowed money.

Besides lending money, banks of today exchange money. That is, they figure out how much the money of one country is worth in another country and then help people from both places exchange one type of money for another. If you're an American who wants to do business in France, for example, you have to change your American dollars for French francs. A bank can help you do that, although it will charge you a fee for each exchange you make.

In ancient times, too, there were people who changed money. As we saw in Chapter 1, the cities of ancient Greece each had their own coins. Money changers exchanged coins from different cities, as well as exchanging coins for gold and silver. Each time they made an exchange, they charged a fee, just like the banks of today.

In both ancient and modern times, this exchange helped make trade easier between different cities and countries. Another important function of banks today is to promote international trade and investments by making it easier to transfer money from one country to another.

The word *bank* comes from an Italian word, *banca*, which is very similar to the word that means "bench." That's because in A.D. 1100, the first European banks began in Italy. Individual bankers changed money, made loans, and did other types of business—all on the street, on small wooden benches. The Italian word for "bank" and for "bench" are the same.

Banks in America

When America was still 13 colonies, its banking system was tied up with that of England. After independence, however, the new country needed a bank of its own. In 1791, the First Bank of the United States was started.

This first bank was both the institution that made the rules for all the other banks and a commercial bank itself—that is, a bank that did all the regular types of bank business. Other banks felt that it was unfair for one bank to both be in business and to make the rules. Eventually, in 1811, the federal government closed the First Bank, and the country depended on state banks.

The state banks also had problems, however. They issued their own *bank notes*—pieces of paper promising to pay out gold or silver. The advantage of bank notes was that the bank could issue more bank notes than the amount of gold and silver it had in its vaults. As long as not too many people tried to exchange their notes for precious metals, the bank could lend out more money than it actually had.

However, if people did try to exchange their bank notes for gold and silver, they soon ran into problems. Most state banks did not have enough precious metals to cover (pay for) all the bank notes they had issued. As a result, bank notes were soon seen as worthless, since they couldn't be exchanged for anything. To rectify the situation, the Second National Bank of the United States was founded in 1816. This bank made sure that the state banks did not issue bank notes that they couldn't cover and that banks didn't loan money to people who probably wouldn't be able to pay it back.

Once again, state banks thought the National Bank was too powerful, so the Second National Bank was closed in 1836.

The United States kept experimenting with different banking systems. In 1838, the Free Banking Act was passed in New York State. This law allowed anyone to start a bank—as long as the person made certain promises, which were written up in a document called a *charter.* These promises had to do with how much money the bank would hold, in order to cover all loans and notes. This idea caught on, and for several years, various states chartered many banks. In 1863, the National Bank Act was passed, allowing the federal government to charter banks as well. Today, we have both state and federal banks.

However, there was still no central agency to oversee banks and make sure that they were operating properly. Finally, in 1913, the Federal Reserve System was set up. It too continues today, making sure that banks operate safely and properly.

There still remained one major problem with America's banks. As we have seen, banks collect money from individuals and corporations in the form of deposits. They then lend out this money or invest it with other corporations.

You might wonder, then, what would happen if all the people with money in a bank asked to take their money out at the same time. How would the bank be able to give them their money if it had lent or invested most of it?

In fact, this is a serious problem for banks. They count on the fact that most people will *not* want to take back their money for a long time once they have deposited it. That leave the banks free to lend or invest this money. If every person—or even many people—do try to withdraw their money at the same time, a bank could *fail,* or go bankrupt. The bank then would have to admit that it doesn't have enough money to cover its obligations.

Bank failures used to be quite common, especially during times of recession or depression. In hard times, businesses or individuals might not pay back their loans. Investments, instead of paying a profit, might turn into giant losses. The money that the bank had loaned out or invested was therefore no longer available to it. If this happened on a big enough scale, the bank might start running low on money. Then, if depositors started asking for their money back, the bank might not be able to honor all of its deposits. As you can imagine, this would be a great hardship on people who had been carefully saving their money for years or to businesses that had put all their money into a bank for safekeeping.

Bank failures were especially common during the Great Depression. When President Franklin D. Roosevelt took office in 1933, one of the first things he did was to close all the banks, so that depositors could not panic and take all their money out. Later the same year, the Federal Deposit Insurance Corporation (FDIC) was set up. This government agency *insures* or guarantees people's deposits up to a certain amount. Because of the FDIC, plus increased prosperity, bank failures were virtually unknown for many years.

Today the nature of banking has changed a great deal. Many other financial institutions lend money, make investments, and perform the types of functions that only banks used to perform. Meanwhile, difficult economic conditions have led to the largest number of bank failures since the

Great Depression. More changes in banking are likely to come during the 1990s.

The Stock Market

Another important institution in our economy is the stock exchange, often called the stock market. When a company wants to attract investors—people who will help provide money for running and expanding its business—it sells *shares of stock*. A share of stock is a percentage of ownership of the company.

Let's say that a business is worth $100,000. And let's say that the business is a *privately held* company—one that is completely owned by a few private individuals or a single corporation. The business owners decide that they want to attract more money from investors so that they can expand their business. They want to turn their business into a *public* company—one in which members of the public can invest.

The owners of the corporation decide to divide their company into 100,000 *shares*, or portions, that they will sell for $1.00 each. As you can see, the price of the total number of shares equals the value of the entire company. Everyone who buys a share is buying a share of the company's *stock*, or value.

There are many different ways a corporation can sell shares. It can do it through a bank, through a financial company, or through a whole range of investment arrangements. The most well-known way to sell shares of stock, however, is to put them up for sale on the stock exchange. There are several stock exchanges around the world. One of the biggest is the New York Stock Exchange, founded in 1790. More than 70 percent of all stock transactions in the United States are handled at the New York Stock Exchange. Some other key stock exchanges include the American Stock Exchange, also in the United States, and the exchanges in London, Tokyo, and Paris.

What happens when a corporation sells stock? Basically, the corporation is selling a percentage of the company. That means that a person who buys stock in the company gets to vote on how it should be run. Votes are divided up according to how much stock a person owns. If one person owns 51 percent of the stock in a company, that person will have 51 percent of the votes. Usually, however, an owner doesn't need 51 percent of a company's stock in order to control a company. So many people, banks, and corporations own stock in so many companies that 10 percent or even less might be enough to control decisions in a company.

A stockholder or shareholder is also entitled to a share of the company's profits. A company spends its profits in many different ways, however. It might use the profits to replace old, broken machinery that doesn't work well any more, or to buy a new, computerized system that might make the company more efficient. It might invest its surplus profits in some other company or even buy up some other business, in order to expand its wealth and power. Sometimes companies use extra profits to raise the salaries of their executives or to give bonuses to their employees.

But at some point, a company will take a certain portion of its profits and pay them out to its stockholders. Once again, the percentage of stock someone owns determines how much of the profit that person gets. Someone whose stock amounts to only 1 percent of the company's total stock will get only 1 percent of the money that the company is paying to its stockholders. Someone who owns 10 percent of the company's stock will get 10 percent of the money.

Once a company puts its stock up for sale, that is not the end of the process. The people who own stock in the company may want to sell their stock to other people. Likewise, new investors may be eager to buy stock in a good company. Since a company can't sell more than 100 percent of its stock, that means that the same shares of stock are sold, or *traded*, back and forth between private individuals, corporations, and banks. These shares of stock are traded on a stock exchange.

How does this work? Every morning, a stock's current price is listed. A person who wants to sell his or her stock might agree to sell at that price. If no one wants to sell at that price, however, a buyer might have to offer more. In that case, the price of a stock will go up. On the other hand, if a person wants to sell stock and no one wants to buy at the price offered, that person might have to lower the price in order to attract more buyers. In that case, the price of a stock will go down.

Many factors go into determining whether a stock's price goes up or down. Here are a few of the most important.

- how a specific segment of the economy is doing (For example, when oil is expensive, oil stock tends to go up, whereas automobile stock tends to go down.)
- how a particular company is doing (Would you rather buy stock in a company that was doing well or one that was doing badly?)
- how much money a company pays out to its investors (Would you rather buy stock in a company that paid you a big amount, or *dividend*, at the end of each year, or one that put more of its money back into buying new machinery and expanding its own business?)
- how investors believe a company will do in the future (If a new law was passed requiring automobiles to use special filters to prevent pollution, what kind of future would you predict for the company that made those filters?)

Because the stock exchange is such a large and complicated institution, individuals are not allowed to trade stocks there themselves. Instead, all trading must be done through registered *brokers*, or traders. An individual, corporation, or bank that owns stock must call up a broker and tell him or her what to do. An owner might say, "I want you to sell my stock, but only if you can get $10 a share for it," or "Buy me some of that American Super Company Stock—I'm willing to pay as much as $50 per share," or "Buy me some stock that you think is a good investment—I've got $1,000 to spend and I'm willing to take your advice."

All of the investment activity on the stock exchange and elsewhere is regulated by a government agency called the Securities and Exchange Commission (SEC). This agency's job is to protect the public from fraud and dishonesty in trading.

Stock Market Highs and Lows

The average price of stock on the New York Stock Exchange is called the *Dow Jones average*. Economists use the Dow Jones as an indicator of how the economy as a whole is doing. Stock prices go up and down depending on many factors. When the stock market goes down—that is, when the price of most of the stocks on the stock market are falling—that may signal problems for the economy as a whole. There are day-to-day changes that do not signal major problems for the economy, but when prices fall drastically in a short period of time or when they continue a steady decline for a long period, the economy may be troubled.

Economists are happy when stock prices go up because it means that people are making money. If you have bought some stock at $10 per share and six months later people are willing to pay $15 per share for it, you can make a profit of $5 per share if you sell your stock. Of course, you may be taking a chance. Perhaps the stock will go up even higher, to $20 a share. If you've already sold it, you've missed your chance to make that extra money. On the other hand, you may be taking a chance by *not* selling. Perhaps tomorrow the price will go down to $9 per share. Then, if you sold your stock, you'd be losing $1 on every share. Generally, traders on the stock exchange want to buy and sell when stocks are at the best possible prices—but no one knows exactly when that time is.

Therefore, although most economists are happy when stock prices go up, there are problems even then. Perhaps many traders are eagerly buying a stock, believing that it will go up in value. The more they believe that stock will go up, the more eager they are to buy it quickly, so that they will own the stock before its value increases. The more eager they are to buy the stock, the more demand there is, and the more the stock's price goes up. Everyone is so eager to buy the stock that they're willing to pay a lot more for it than normal, because they believe that the price is going to go up even higher.

But there comes a time when stock prices just can't go up any more. People stop being optimistic about the future and decide that they want to sell their stock and get their money *now.* As people become more eager to sell a stock than to buy it, the stock's price starts going down. Sometime this sets off a panic. People see a stock price going down and think, "Oh, no, my stock is falling in value. I'd better sell it now before its price goes any lower." The more people think this, the more they are eager to sell, and stock prices keep going lower and lower. People tell their brokers, "I'd rather take a lower price and get my money. I'm afraid that if I hold onto my stock, the price will never go back up again. Since the price is going down, sell now before it goes down further."

When this happens, the Dow Jones average falls. If it falls fast enough, we say that the stock market has "crashed." The last time the market crashed was in October 1987. For many years, the market had been rising and many people had been making lots of money. Then the process turned around, and suddenly many people, along with banks, corporations, and other businesses, lost millions of dollars as stock prices dropped almost overnight. People and businesses had taken all their extra money to invest in stock, believing that they could always get their money back again by selling the stock. But when stock prices fell below what people had originally paid, they realized they would not get their money back. Stock that they had bought for, say, $100 a share was now worth only $50 a share, and it looked as though prices would never go back up to where they had been before.

Although the stock market has improved since then, many businesses closed or cut back severely as a result of the crash. The economy suffered and is still recovering. However, as bad as the crash of 1987 was, it was not nearly as bad as the great stock market crash of 1929. Throughout the 1920s, stock prices had been going up. People borrowed huge sums of money to buy stock, believing that they could get rich by doing so. When the market crashed in October 1929, hundreds of thousands of people and businesses lost their money. Suddenly they had huge debts that they had no way of paying. This was the beginning of the Great Depression, which lasted throughout the 1930s, until the United States entered World War II in 1941.

The Government and the Economy

So far, we've focused mainly on the private institutions in our economy: corporations, banks, and the stock market. However, the government, or *public sector*, is also a very important part of the economy.

The government affects the economy in many important ways. Here are a few:

- It maintains the roads, bridges, and airports that businesses use to transport goods and people from place to place.
- It buys billions of dollars' worth of goods and services from many different private corporations, including those who make military hardware and those who construct schools, libraries, and other public buildings.

- It employs hundreds of thousands of people, as government workers and in the military.
- It provides money to those who are unemployed, via welfare payments, food stamps, and other social programs. (Social Security and unemployment insurance are two programs that are regulated by the government but paid for by individual contributions, rather than by tax dollars.)
- It regulates business activity through laws, and through agencies such as the Securities and Exchange Commission and the Federal Reserve system.
- It taxes people and businesses to pay for all those other activities, and this affects how much money these people and businesses have left to spend on other things.

Before the Great Depression of 1929, the United States government was far less involved in business activities than it is today. It also had far fewer social programs. Welfare was virtually unknown. Social Security and unemployment insurance did not exist. There were no public medical plans such as Medicare or Medicaid. If a person lost his or her job, he or she simply had no money coming in until another job could be found. A person might literally starve or become homeless, with no help to be found except from a few private charities.

Then, after the depression began, about one-third of the work force was out of work. Something had to be done to deal with this crisis—especially since people who are out of work can't afford to buy very much. A vicious cycle had begun: with so many people unable to buy anything, businesses had trouble selling their products, and they in turn had to fire more people, creating still more unemployment.

When Franklin D. Roosevelt took office as president in 1933, he pushed through a great many social programs designed to help people who had no jobs and no money. Welfare, or "relief" as it was then called, was designed to help people through the rough times—and to keep them buying products so that businesses could continue to sell their wares. Roosevelt also got the federal government to engage in many *public works*—public projects such as building new post offices and repairing old sidewalks. These government-financed projects hired many people, enabling them to live decent lives, stay in their homes—and again, continue to buy the products that businesses were selling.

Roosevelt began a trend in which the federal government was expected to provide a "safety net" for those who needed it. During the presidency of Ronald Reagan, this trend was reversed to a great extent. President Reagan believed that the United States could no longer afford social programs of the type begun by Roosevelt, and he tried to cut them back as far as possible. Many people believed that Reagan's actions strengthened the economy a great deal. Others believe that he created enormous poverty and suffering and that the economy will eventually suffer for it, too. Once again, the debate over the government's role in the economy will likely continue throughout the 1990s.

Part II

MONEY AND YOU

3

Messages About Money

On one level, money is simply one factor in a person's life. Having money can be seen simply in practical terms: if you have it, you can buy certain things; if you don't, you can't. Looked at in this way, money problems don't seem very complicated or even very important.

If only it were always that simple! But, of course, it isn't—because having money and the things that money buys has taken on all sorts of other meanings in our society. How many of the following attitudes do you recognize? How many do you share? How many do you believe that members of your family, friends, or others in your community share?

- A person who can't provide for his or her family must be a failure.
- The coolest kids have the nicest clothes.
- People who don't dress well are revealing that they have a low opinion of themselves.
- If my friends treat me, I have to treat them—otherwise, I'm ungrateful and cheap.
- A good friend gives great presents, no matter how much they cost.

- Good people spend money on their friends and their relatives—not on themselves.
- If someone gives you a great present, you'd better give back one that costs at least as much.
- A guy who can't pay for a girl on a date must be a real creep or a nerd.
- If a girl offers to pay for herself on a date, she'll make the guy feel bad, or she'll seem like she's trying to take over.
- If you feel bad, buying a present for yourself is one way to feel better.
- One way that parents can show they love their kids is to buy them nice clothes and other presents.
- If you really want something, money shouldn't stand in your way; people who say they can't afford things are just making excuses.
- A person who can't afford to do things along with his or her friends just isn't much fun.

All of these attitudes reveal that in our society, money is used to give messages that go far beyond "can afford" or "can't afford." Money is used as an indicator of many things: success, love, friendship, treating a date well, being cool or popular, self-esteem (feeling good about yourself), power, and probably a whole host of other qualities besides!

The first step to unraveling the messages about money in our society is to become aware of them. Once you're aware of the messages you've been getting from your family, friends, and neighbors, as well as from advertising, television, the movies, and the political climate of the times, you can start to think through your own values about money.

Money and Politics

As the political climate changes, ideas about money change as well. Different political theories suggest different ways of viewing money, poverty, wealth, society, and the individual.

Here are some of the key theories that have prevailed over the past 20 or 30 years. Although some political thinkers may take ideas from more than one theory, these are the general positions that have evolved in the United States. As you can see, each theory sends a different message about money.

Conservative

According to conservative thinkers, individuals are basically completely responsible for themselves. Although some social "safety nets" like welfare payments to the poor or Medicaid payments to the elderly may be necessary to keep people from the worst consequences of poverty, it's better to let people work out problems on their own as much as possible.

Conservative thinkers tend to believe that, if left alone, the U.S. economic system is basically able to provide for everyone who is willing to work hard. Therefore, if people are poor or unemployed, it's most likely their own fault. Perhaps they're not willing to work hard enough, or maybe they haven't been wise about getting the right kind of education or training. Possibly, according to this philosophy, a person is poor because he or she is lazy, irresponsible, or just not very smart. According to conservative political thinking, there is a certain amount of shame in accepting help for economic problems because the fact that a person needs help suggests that he or she has failed in some way.

Conservative political thinking also believes in giving the greatest possible freedom to the owners of businesses and corporations, on the theory that this freedom leaves the owners free to make the smartest possible business decisions and therefore to run their companies as efficiently as possible. If this means that a plant has to close or greatly reduce its work force or that an employer has to drastically reduce wages, conservatives would argue that this freedom must be allowed, even if it hurts the employees in a community. If a great number of plants close in one area, such as the Northeast, then conservatives believe that the workers in that area should move to another part of the United States where there are more jobs, such as California or the Southwest.

This theory about freedom of the owners of a plant or business gives another message about money. That is, that owning large sums of money or large amounts of property entitles a person to virtually complete freedom in how he or she uses that money or that property. The conservative way of thinking also gives the message that if a person has gotten rich, it's probably because of hard work, skill, or some other good quality, whereas if a person has remained poor, it reflects badly on that person.

Liberal

The liberal way of thinking has traditionally focused on the need to help those who have problems in our current economic system. Social programs such as unemployment insurance, Social Security for the elderly, welfare payments and medical assistance for the poor, and national health insurance for everyone are currently supported by many who would call themselves liberals. Their thinking is that every person in a society has the right to certain benefits and that there's no shame in being poor. Rather than holding each individual responsible for how much money he or she earns, liberals focus on society's responsibility to take care of all of its members.

According to liberal ways of thinking, the way our economic system functions is not always fair or just to everyone. Therefore, the government—society as a whole—needs to step in to correct the worst injustices. One way of doing this is to spend tax money on social programs that help people to get an education, improve their standard of living, or merely to survive. Another way of doing this is to restrict the freedom of employers, such as by requiring them to pay a minimum wage or to recognize the right of employees to form unions that can push for higher salaries. The message this gives about money is that sometimes having money makes people selfish and that sometimes people who don't have money need protection from those who do.

Liberal political thinkers would argue that there are many reasons that people in our society are poor, including racial discrimination, discrimination on the basis of sex, and poor business decisions made by corporate owners. Therefore, in liberal political theory, there is no shame in accepting help from government programs, since poverty is not the individual's fault in the first place. In this way of thinking, lack of money doesn't say anything bad about an individual—it only means that some people sometimes need help.

Like conservatives, liberal political thinkers generally support great freedom for the owners of businesses and corporations. However, some liberals would argue that these owners should also bear some responsibility along with their great power. Therefore, many liberals would support such policies as higher taxes on the rich, with the money going to support programs to help the poor. Other liberals would go further, arguing that corporations' actions should be restricted in various ways, since corporate owners cannot always be trusted to act in the interest of society as a whole.

Some liberals, for example, might favor the government giving emergency economic assistance to the people living in a community where a plant has closed. Others might favor requiring a plant to give two years' notice to a community before it closes, or to pay employees' moving costs as they travel to other parts of the country, or to pay for retraining for those workers who want to qualify for other jobs. Whatever the remedy a liberal might propose, he or she would point out that an individual employee has no control over a plant closing and that individuals might suffer great economic hardship or even poverty through no fault of their own. Once again, the message about money here is that there is no shame in not having money—only hardship. Therefore, either the people who do have money or the government should step in and ease the burdens that come with poverty.

Radical

Liberal and conservative political theories both agree that private ownership of property is the most efficient way to run an economy. Both agree that private owners should have a great deal of freedom in using their property and running their businesses as they see fit. Liberals and conservatives may disagree about how much responsibility the rich have for the poor or about how easy it is to break out of poverty in this country—but they do tend to agree that basically, the system of private ownership is a good thing and that having money is the reward of hard work and dedication.

Radical political theory disagrees with this basic premise. There are many different types of radical political theories, each proposing different models for how a society should be run. In fact, there is a great deal of disagreement among radicals about how best to run an economy efficiently and fairly.

Where radicals do agree, however, is in their basic attitude that much about the U.S. economy is profoundly unfair. According to this theory, there is no shame at all in not having money; in fact, the economic system is set up in such a way that a certain amount of poverty is virtually guaranteed. According to many radical political thinkers, in fact, there is almost a kind of shame in *having* money, since a rich person probably became wealthy at someone else's expense and now enjoys power and privilege that are unfairly denied to other people.

Both radicals and liberals would agree that there are many factors in our society that keep certain people—especially racial minorities and women—from achieving full economic equality. Liberals, however, would say that these factors can be corrected through government programs and through an increased awareness on the part of all citizens who are willing to do something about social problems. Radicals would say that as long as a few wealthy corporations are allowed full freedom to make profits—as long as individuals are allowed to focus their efforts on getting rich—inevitably, many other people are going to be hurt.

In our example about the plant closing, for instance, radical political theory would say that a corporate owner has no right to make a decision that hurts so many people in a community. A radical would point out that closing a plant throws many people out of work and hurts the economy of an entire area, including all the stores, schools, libraries, and other businesses that depend upon the income from that plant. While liberals and conservatives would agree that a plant owner has the right to do whatever is best for his or her business, radicals would say that the rights of workers and the community must also be taken into account. Radicals might propose that communities should have the right to vote on whether or not plants should close, or that companies that close plants should put a great deal of money into the communities they leave to help them recuperate from the blow.

As you can see, each of the three political theories gives a different message about money:

Conservative: Having money means you have worked hard and made intelligent decisions, whereas not having money means you have not taken full advantage of all the opportunities in the U.S. economy. Having money means you have earned the right to use your money as you see fit, which will probably also benefit the economy as a whole, since you will continue to make the intelligent business decisions that made you rich in the first place.

Liberal: Having money probably means you have made intelligent business decisions, and basically you should be given the freedom to keep on making them. However, not having money is not necessarily a person's own fault. Many factors get in the way of a person's economic success, and society as a whole should help people who are having a difficult time.

Radical: Having money probably means that you have taken advantage of other people. Having money or owning a corporation should not give a person the right to make decisions—such as closing a plant or laying people off—that greatly affect the lives of many other people. People who don't have money aren't to blame for their own difficulties; they are merely suffering from the inevitable consequences of the self-interested activities of corporations and big business.

Money and Popular Images

Another place we get messages about money is from movies, television, advertising, and other popular images. Although we may not realize it as we watch a movie or walk past a billboard, we are getting many different messages about money—message that may affect the way we think and feel about money, our families, and ourselves.

One popular image of money is that "everybody has it." Most popular images focus on people with lots of money—well-dressed people living in big houses with plenty of expensive possessions. It would be easy to get the impression from popular images that "everybody is rich" or that it's unusual to have to struggle to make ends meet.

If your family or your community is not like the ones pictured in popular images, it would be easy to get the impression that you were the "odd one out." Of course, most people don't live at the level pictured in television, movies, or advertisements. But there is something about the power of these images that makes it seem as though they are the norm and everything else is the exception, even though the facts of your own life may suggest a different reality.

Another strong message about money in popular images is that it doesn't make any difference whether you have it or not. That is, all the real strains of not having money—the family arguments, the difficult choices, the real limits that might be placed on someone's education—are ignored or glossed over. Situation comedies about "ordinary families" may show comic situations in which a parent is worried about bills or a child is angry about not being able to afford a new jacket, but these are very far from the actual money problems that most families experience. Even though you and your family may know enough not to take television too seriously, you may be absorbing a message about money without realizing it—a message that makes you or your family feel to blame for having such a difficult time when the people on television are obviously not having the same kinds of problems.

At the other extreme, television or movie dramas may portray all poor people as criminals, vicious, or from unloving families. The message here might be that having money means you can have a happy, loving family life, whereas not having money means that you are condemned to terrible relationships even with those you love.

Here is a list of some other messages that may be given about money by television, movies, and advertisements. Can you think of times you've seen something that gives one of these messages?

- Buying things or having things makes people happy.
- Looking fashionable and wearing the latest styles is really important.
- One way you can tell who is cool and who isn't is by the things a person owns and the clothes a person wears.
- Nobody has to work very hard to have nice things.
- It's possible both to have a lot of nice things and to have lots of free time to spend with your family.
- Nobody has to worry much about getting old, getting sick, paying for a college education, or losing a job.
- People who do have to worry about those things can usually find simple solutions to their problems.
- There is usually a good reason why one person has money and another doesn't; there's nothing unfair about it.

How many other messages like this can you think of?

Money and Friends

The messages about money that affect you the most on a daily basis are probably the messages that come from your friends. Messages about money from friends are some of the hardest messages to deal with. That's because in our society, it's usually not considered polite to talk about money. Therefore, although money is extremely important, it is the subject of a lot of hidden messages. And hidden messages are much more difficult to deal with than messages that are spoken directly. When you get a hidden message, you have to figure out what it is before you can even start to deal with it. You may be given one message in words and another, hidden message in actions or tone of voice, so that you have to believe in yourself and your own perceptions in order to deal effectively with the hidden message. However, if you can learn to identify the hidden messages that you're getting about money from your friends, you'll probably find that they're much easier to deal with.

Sometimes, of course, you're not actually getting hidden messages from your friends about money—but you feel uncomfortable about money anyway. That's because we all have our own fears and anxieties about our friends as well as about money—and sometimes the two areas get mixed up!

Here are some examples of situations in which there are hidden messages and mixed feelings about money. Do any of them sound like situations that you recognize?

Jean's friends like to hang out at the mall on Saturdays and sometimes after school. The mall is a great place to meet other kids, and there's so much to do there! But Jean always notices how expensive it is: she and her friends usually stop and get something to eat, sometimes several times; they always stop by the record store and buy the latest CDs; they usually check out the cosmetics counter, the jewelry store, and a few other places to buy clothes. Jean worries that if she hangs out but doesn't buy anything, she'll feel left out or like a hanger-on. Also, the store clerks always give kids a dirty look, so you have to buy things or they make you feel really low.

J. J. wants to ask Leonie out, but he's afraid that if he doesn't pay for everything, she won't take him seriously. Maybe she'll even be insulted. He thinks he's solved the problem by saving enough money for a movie and a snack afterward, but then he starts worrying—what if she wants more than a snack? How can he say "no," or "let's each pay," without seeming like he doesn't care about her, or looking like a baby, or just turning her off? On the other hand, if he waits till he's saved enough money for a really expensive date, she might already have started going out with some-body else. Even if he does manage to take her on one expensive date, how long will he have to wait before he can afford the next one?

Meanwhile, Leonie would really like to go out with J. J., and she can't understand why he hasn't asked her. She has somehow gotten the impression that he might be worried about money, and she'd like to let him know that she doesn't care who pays or what they do, but she doesn't know how to do this without insulting him. She's afraid J. J. has the same idea as most guys she knows—that it's the guy's responsi-bility to pay on a date, and that a girl who offers to pay is making it look like she thinks the guy can't handle it. In fact, Leonie would really like to ask J. J. out herself, but she's afraid to do that—she thinks that he still might feel it was his place to pay, and if she asks him out, she'll be forcing him to spend money on her.

Tanya is invited to her friend Sara's birthday party. For Tanya's birthday, Sara gave her a beautiful silk scarf. Tanya is sure that it must have cost at least 20 dollars—which is a lot more money than Tanya could ever spend on a present.

She doesn't want Sara to think she's cheap or doesn't like her, but she doesn't know how to match Sara's present. To make matters worse, she's heard about some of the presents Sara's other friends are planning to buy, and all of them cost more than Tanya can afford. She doesn't want to be the only one at the party with a cheap present—but she also doesn't want to borrow on the next four months of her allowance just to buy Sara a gift.

Sara, meanwhile, is feeling uncomfortable about asking Tanya to her party because she knows that Tanya doesn't have much money and she's worried that Tanya will feel out of place. Sara really likes Tanya, but she knows that she has a lot more money that Tanya does, and often it's hard to invite Tanya to join her because she knows Tanya won't be able to afford to do the same things her other friends can. It makes Sara angry and confused to think she should have to cut back on her own activities just because Tanya can't afford them—but if she offers to pay for Tanya, that only seems to make things worse: Tanya either gets very huffy and says there's no need, or she accepts and then seems to act very grateful and quiet, as though she has no right to have any opinion of her own about anything if Sara is paying.

Ernesto comes from a very large family that lives in a very small apartment. His older brother sleeps on the living room couch, and since he's a night security guard, he's often sleeping or just getting up when Ernesto gets home from school. Ernesto would like to invite his friends home sometimes, instead of always going to their houses, but he knows his house is smaller and poorer than his friends', and he just isn't sure how they would feel about him after they see how he lives. He isn't sure whether they would make fun of him, feel sorry for him, or just be surprised— but he hates the idea of any of those reactions. He just wants to be normal, with a regular big house and no one on the couch, like everybody else.

What are some of the messages that the people in these situations are picking up? Rightly or wrongly, they are operating as though these were the hidden messages in their situations:

- If you can't afford the things your friends can afford, you don't belong.
- A guy always has to buy a girl anything she wants.
- A girl who pays for herself—or for her date—is insulting a guy.
- If you can't give your friend as good a present as he or she gave you, then you are failing as a friend.
- If someone treats you, you give up your right to have an opinion of your own.
- You can never talk openly about someone having more money than someone else.
- There's something wrong with having less money than other people.

Can you identify any other messages in these situations? To what extent are these messages really being sent, and to what extent are people simply imagining them?

Coping with Friends and Money

What types of solutions are there for the problems in the situations we just discussed? Of course, every situation is different, and usually there is more than one solution for each problem. Here are some ways that the people in these situations *might* have coped with their problems:

Jean might tell her friends that she can't afford to spend as much money as they do, but that she'd like to spend time with them anyway. She might say something like, "Hey, guys, I don't get much allowance and I really can't buy something every single day. I'd like to hang out with you anyway, but I don't want to feel like I have to buy something all the time."

Jean might also figure out how much she'd like to spend and stick to her limit, such as buying only a drink when her friends stop for a snack, or buying only a single lipstick instead of buying a CD *and* a piece of jewelry *and* a cosmetic. She might ask her friends to alternate going to the mall with some other activity that doesn't cost as much—or she might find other friends to spend time with as well as going to the mall with her shopping friends.

J. J. might tell Leonie directly that he'd like to spend time with her, but that he doesn't have much money. He could suggest either doing inexpensive things, sharing expenses equally, or sharing expenses unequally, such as him paying for the meal in a restaurant while Leonie leaves the tip, or him paying for the movie while Leonie buys the popcorn. He might say something like, "Leonie, I'd like to ask you out, but I don't have much money right now. Can we do something that doesn't cost much money?" or "Can we each pay for ourselves?" or "How about if I pay for the movie and you get the popcorn?" or "How about if we go to a movie but just go for a walk afterward instead of going to a restaurant?" He might also ask Leonie how she would like to handle the situation: "I'd really like to take you out, but I don't have much money right now. What do you think we should do about that?"

J. J. might also find things to do that don't cost much, such as a walk in the park, a visit to a museum, or a day at a fair or festival. A little research in the local newspapers and magazines or with the Chamber of Commerce might turn up some interesting activities.

For her part, Leonie might tell J. J. directly that she'd like to spend time with him. She then has a lot of options: she can ask him how he'd like to handle the money; she can offer to pay for herself; she can offer to pay for both of them half the time; she can point out that she likes to do things that don't cost much money and she could make a few suggestions. She might say, "I'd love to go out with you, J. J., but I don't want you to think you've got to spend a lot of money. Why don't I pay for myself ?" or "Why don't we take turns paying?" or "Let's find stuff to do that doesn't cost much, because I don't want money to be a reason that we don't see each other."

Leonie could also find a way to ask J. J. out to do something that doesn't cost much money—a walk in the park, a visit to a museum, having a soda together, or attending some free local event.

Tanya could consider making a gift or a card for Sara that show a lot of time and attention. Or she could invent a gift that has to do with time and energy rather than money, such as a "gift certificate" offering "three hours of help with your least favorite chore" or "taking care of your little brother two different times."

If Tanya is concerned about how her gift will be perceived, she could talk with Sara or write her a note about how important the friendship is to Tanya, so that it's clear that the friendship and the cost of the gift are not related. She might also talk with Sara about her uncomfortable feelings concerning money. Tanya might say something like, "I'd really like to come to your birthday party, Sara, but I feel a little uncomfortable because I know your other friends will be giving you expensive gifts and right now I just can't afford to do that. You're a good friend and I want to be there, and I don't want you to think that I'm not spending money because I don't like you—I just don't have it."

Before going to the party, Tanya could remind herself that there are lots of ways of showing friendship besides spending money. This might help her to focus on her feelings of friendship for *Sara*, rather than on her feelings of shame and embarrassment concerning Sara's other friends.

Sara, on the other hand, could share with Tanya her own feelings of discomfort and frustration about money.

She might say something like, "I really like doing things with you, but it's hard sometimes when you get uncomfortable about not having money. I'm really happy to pay for you or I wouldn't offer, but you seem to get uncomfortable about it. What do you think we should do?" Or she might say, "I really like doing things with you, Tanya, but I don't know how to handle it when I want to do something that you can't afford. How do you feel? What do you think we should do?"

If Sara is uncomfortable about the idea of this conversation, she might write Tanya a note about how she feels about Tanya's friendship. This might help both of them separate the issue of friendship from the issue of money.

Ernesto might find that it helps to tell his friends about the situation at home, so that he can separate getting their reaction from actually having them inside his house. He might say something like, "Boy, it's really crowded at my house. Besides all the rest of us who live there, my older brother is sleeping on the couch every day—he works all night and sleeps all day!" That way, he can get some of his friends' reactions to the situation without actually being inside his house or with his family, which might make it easier to judge their reactions honestly instead of defensively.

At the same time, Ernesto could remind himself that every family has problems. His family's problem may be easy to spot because it has to do with money, but his friends' families also have problems, even if he can't see them just by visiting.

Ernesto might bring home just one friend at a time, after talking with the friend about what his house is like. That way, it will be easier not to get overwhelmed by anybody's reaction or by his own feelings of nervousness and discomfort.

What other ways of coping can you think of?

What Makes It Difficult to Cope

What gets in the way of doing these things? Why is it so difficult to talk honestly with friends about money, or even to think clearly about these issues ourselves?

As we've seen in this chapter, society is full of messages about money, and most of these messages are hidden messages. Nobody stands up on a television show and says, "Everybody should be living like this, and if you don't you don't count." Nobody comes right out in an advertisement and says, "The people who can afford this product are happy and the ones who can't afford it are miserable." Most people won't say in so many words, "I'll love you if you buy me an expensive present, and I'll get tired of you if you don't." Whether these messages are actually coming through or we only think they're coming through, they can be painful and difficult to deal with precisely because they are so hidden.

There are also a lot of rules in our society about not mentioning money. You're not supposed to ask how much something costs, how much money someone earns, or how much rent they pay. These rules suggest that there is something embarrassing or shameful about money—particularly about not having money!

These rules might also make it difficult even to face the truth within ourselves. Ernesto doesn't want to admit even to himself that he's embarrassed about his parents' home or his brother's sleeping on the couch—what kind of son does it make him if he's ashamed of his family? Sara doesn't like acknowledging that she has more money than Tanya or that she gets impatient when Tanya can't afford something—does that mean she's a snob or a bad friend? Tanya doesn't want to face the fact that she can't afford as expensive a gift as Sara's other friends can give her—does that make her a failure? J. J. and Leonie are uncomfortable talking about how to handle money on their dates—it's hard enough just going out with someone, let alone talking about who's going to pay! Jean doesn't like having to tell her friends that she can't afford to do what they take for granted—she already feels different and left out sometimes, and she doesn't want to feel like any more of an outsider.

Sometimes it's helpful just to admit that money issues *are* often painful, difficult, embarrassing, and lonely. Figuring out how to handle money and how to handle its impact on our relationships is one of the hardest jobs that an adult has to do. As you get older and take on more adult pleasures and responsibilities—such as dating, earning money, shopping, and spending time with friends away from your parents' supervision—you are bound to find yourself dealing with some of the same difficult adult issues.

The good news is that these issues can be faced, and facing them does make things easier, even if it doesn't completely solve the problem. The more honestly and bravely you can face your own feelings about money and the messages about money that you receive, the easier it will be for you to act in ways that are satisfying and comfortable to you. And the more practice you get in handling these issues now, the better you'll be at dealing with them as you mature.

4

Ways to Earn
Money

One way to deal with money issues is to earn some money of your own. You can earn money in several different ways: by getting a job—waiter or waitress, clerk in a store, paper deliverer; by performing a service for people in your community—babysitting, yard work, housecleaning, errands; or by making and selling something that people want to buy—crafts, items of clothing, baked goods, woodwork, or the like.

There are lots of advantages to earning your own money. These include: a sense of accomplishment, practice in the work world, learning how to get along with different types of people and in different types of situations, the freedom to spend your own money in your own way, learning more about who you are and what you can do, and, of course, more money!

There are also some responsibilities and possible disadvantages that go along with earning your own money. You may have less free time and more obligations, and you may need to plan your life more carefully. There may be strains on schoolwork, family relations, and relations with your friends, as well as whatever strains and stresses come with the job or way of earning money that you have found.

If, on balance, you think that earning more of your own money is the right choice for you, read on! This chapter will give you suggestions for how to find a job or earn money in some other way, as well as helping you think through your rights and responsibilities on the job.

Child Labor and Your Protection

Before you take on a job or some other way of earning money, you will probably need to get your parents' permission. Your parents will probably be concerned that you not overwork yourself, that you allow time for your schoolwork, and that you not enter into any situations that might be dangerous or overwhelming. (Parents may have other concerns about your earning money as well. For more on this topic, see Chapter 6, "Money and Families.") Most employers will probably want to know that you have your parents' permission to take a job; some may even require a letter or a signed form.

Many years ago, there were no age restrictions on employment. Children of any age could work at any job that an employer was willing to hire them for. Children as young as five and six years old worked at dirty, dangerous jobs, such as mining, where they were employed to go into tunnels too small for adults to enter. Children were often hired out to live with other families as servants if their own families couldn't afford to keep them. Nobody protected these children's health and safety, let alone made sure that they had time to rest and play—or that they got a decent education. Many families needed the income from these child laborers in order to survive.

To stop this oppressive situation, child labor laws were passed restricting the types and amount of work that children of certain ages could do. One reason for child labor laws was simply to protect children. Another was the belief that if children were not allowed to work, employers would have to hire adults at higher wages, so that families would no longer need to depend on the income of children.

As a result of the movement against child labor, there are currently many laws that restrict the circumstances under which children can work. These laws may be frustrating to you now, but they grew out of a situation that was far more restrictive and dangerous to children than any work-related situation that exists today.

Finding and Getting Work

The first step in getting work is to identify the kind of work that you can get. Here are some of the jobs that a young person is likely to be hired for:

- counterperson, waiter, or waitress
- dishwasher
- store clerk
- babysitter
- paper boy or paper girl
- service station attendant
- stock person at a store or fruit stand (carrying things, doing errands, cleaning up)
- farm worker (especially for seasonal work like hoeing sugar beets or harvesting fruit)

There are lots of different ways to get these different jobs.

Answering an Advertisement

The easiest way of getting work is for someone to offer you a job. An advertisement is the next best thing to a job offer. It lets you know that an employer needs help and is planning to hire at least one person.

You can find ads for employment in all sorts of places. Daily and weekly newspapers usually run want ads—ads from employers who want to hire someone. You might find an ad from a store or a restaurant that is willing to hire a young person. If there is a college in your area, college employees might advertise for babysitters or other types of student help in the college newspaper. Even if the advertiser is looking for someone of college-student age, you might be able to convince the person that you, too, can be a responsible babysitter or household helper.

Frequently, bulletin boards at grocery stores, libraries, community centers, video stores, and other popular places have ads from people who are looking for babysitters, household help, or yard help. Individuals who put up such advertisements are probably your best bet for work, since they are most likely to be willing to hire a younger person.

Of course, sometimes employers run ads that attract tens or even hundreds more people than they can possibly hire. Sometimes, too, employers misrepresent a job in an ad. They might write "Great possibilities for advancement" when they're talking about going from the night shift to the day shift in a janitorial job. Or they might write, "Salary depends on you!" when what they really mean is that as a waiter or waitress, you'll be depending on tips for most of your income.

Also, employers might not specify which age groups they are looking for in an ad. They may assume that everyone who applies will be an adult, or at least over 16. People who are looking for work often find themselves frustrated by want ads that sound promising but turn out to offer nothing.

So the first thing to remember about looking at ads is not to get discouraged. The second thing to remember is to read the ad carefully. Exactly what is the employer asking for? Sometimes the ad mentions age. If you are much younger than the age being mentioned, you may not have much chance of being hired. There may even be legal reasons why you can't be. On the other hand, an employer who will hire an older teenager might very well be willing to hire a younger teen, once he or she has met you and seen how responsible you are.

Sometimes the ad will say "experienced only." Again, this doesn't necessarily mean that you shouldn't apply—but it does mean that you should be aware that the employer is looking for a particular type of person. If you go to apply for your first waiter or waitress job when the ad has asked for "experienced waiters only," you should at least let the employer know that you've read the ad. You might offer to work on a short trial basis to prove that you can overcome your lack of experience in a short time: "I know your ad said 'experienced only,' but I learn fast and I'm really good with people. Why don't you try me out for a day or two, and if I work out, we've both gained something."

Placing an Advertisement

Another way of getting work is to place your own advertisement to say that you are looking for certain types of employment—usually babysitting, mother's helper, yard work, housecleaning, and the like. If you can afford it, you might pay for an ad in a local newspaper or magazine. Or you might post your ad at libraries, grocery stores, community centers, and other places that have bulletin boards. You might check out these bulletin boards to see what kinds of ads other people in your situation have put up.

A good advertisement should say something about who you are, what you are willing to do, and how you can be reached. It should at least mention the qualities that a prospective employer will be looking for—"reliable" or "likes children" if you want to babysit; "efficient" or "speedy" if you're trying to get housework or yard work.

If you have *references*—people for whom you have worked before or respectable people who know you and will vouch for your honesty and efficiency—you can mention that fact: "References available upon request." (You should check with the person you want to use as a reference *before* you give his or her name out.) Likewise, if you have special qualifications for your job—if you've taken a course in first aid for babysitters, for example—you should mention that. Mention anything that you think would interest someone or get them to call.

If you have very definite ideas about how much you intend to charge, you should give that information in your ad, especially if you think your rates are low or average for your area. If, however, you are willing to negotiate or to consider different arrangements, don't put your fees in your ad, since it might discourage some people from calling you. Likewise, if there is a particular time of day you are available for, you might mention that, to save yourself from getting calls from people who will ask you to work at times that you aren't available.

Here are some sample ads that teenagers might write to get work:

RELIABLE BABYSITTER—
EVENINGS AND WEEKENDS

I love children and would love to take care of yours. Reliable, experienced babysitter (four younger brothers and sisters!) is eager to work for you. Reasonable rates—references available upon request. Call Chris, 555-1234.

TIRED OF SHOVELING SNOW
AND RAKING LEAVES?

Let me do it for you! For less money than you might expect, I can take care of the yard work that you would rather not do. Call Sandy at 555-6788—I'll be happy to give you the names of other satisfied customers!

MOTHER'S HELPER SEEKS WORK

I am willing to do any type of housework or childcare. Available after school and on weekends. We can work out a price.

Pat—555-9245

Approaching Possible Employers

Sometimes the best way for teenagers and pre-teens to get jobs is simply to make the rounds of all possible employers, especially during the time when they're most likely to be hiring—before summer and in the months before Christmas. Stores, restaurants, and fast-food places all do much more business in those times, and they also lose college students and other employees who tend to move or leave town for Christmas and summer holidays. Even if a place of business hasn't advertised for employees, they may keep your application on file and when something turns up, they may call you.

If you decide to make the rounds in this way, you should show up dressed neatly and appropriately. You want to be dressed in such a way that an employer could say, "OK, you're hired. Why don't you start work right now?" Although this is very unlikely to happen, dressing as though it could shows a prospective employer that you understand his or her needs as far as cleanliness, dress code, and style are concerned. If you're not sure how to dress, make a quick trip to the places you're applying to before you apply. Notice how the salespeople, counterpeople, or waiters are dressed. If they are wearing uniforms, notice how the manager is dressed. If everyone is in uniform, choose your most conservative outfit to apply for work—no jeans, shorts, workshirts, short skirts, or outrageous styles. Of course, it goes without saying that you show up clean, with clean hair! Girls should go easy on makeup, perfume, and jewelry—you want to convey that you're ready for work, not for a playful Saturday afternoon or a date.

Of course, if you're applying for farm work, yard work, work at a service station, or some other kind of job that requires heavy physical labor or getting dirty, you might want to dress appropriately for *that* job. In that case, wear clean work clothes—again, the kind of clothes that would be appropriate to wear if the manager said to you, "Why don't you work a couple of hours right now so we can see how you'll work out."

You should also show up ready to fill out any applications that a business might give you. Usually you'll be asked basic information—name, address, phone number, Social Security number—as well as where you go to school, last grade completed, and other work experience. If you have any work experience, even babysitting or yard work for neighbors, put it down as though it were a regular job. That means having the names, addresses, and phone numbers of the people you've worked for, so that you can put them on the application where it says "former employers." Of course, if you've babysat or done work for six or seven people, don't put them all down. Just choose one or two who you know will give you good recommendations if they get called. It's a good idea to ask these people if you can use their names before you go to apply for work.

An application that asks about former employers usually also asks why you left the job. You might write "Still do occasional work for them," or "They didn't need help any more," if you are describing someone you babysat or did yard work for.

You'll probably also be asked for references. Sometimes this section specifies that references should be "personal references"—people whom you have *not* worked for and who are not related to you. You should speak to one or two adults to confirm that you can use their names in this way. The references section of an application usually asks for name, address, phone number, relation to you or how you know the person, and sometimes the person's type of employment. Some possible sources for personal references include teachers, coaches, ministers, and scout leaders, among others.

Many people find it helpful to write neatly all the information that they might need on a sheet of paper that they can then pull out and copy when they have to fill out a job application. Of course, it goes without saying that you should write as neatly as possible on the application itself. If you don't understand something on an application, ask the person who gave it to you. If something doesn't quite seem to apply, it's all right to write a short note explaining what you mean.

Asking Around

Sometimes the best way to find work is simply to tell as many people as possible that you're looking. Besides visiting all the businesses where you think you could work, tell every person you know, adult or teen, that you're looking for work. Ask every person you know if they have any ideas about how you might earn money.

Sometimes school counselors have ideas for work possibilities. Friends of your parents might also come up with something. Someone who runs a business might know of someone else who needs help, even if he or she doesn't. It usually pays to ask for help in two or three different ways. If a person says that he or she doesn't have any work for you, ask, "Do you know anyone who might need someone?" or "Where do you think I should go next?" or "Do you know anyone who might have any ideas for me?" Asking a person for work is very different from asking him or her to give you a few minutes of creative thought about where you might find work. Sometimes people are happy to help you solve a problem, even if they can't solve it for you themselves.

It also helps to be creative in thinking of what you might do. If you go into a neighborhood store, for example, it might not be realistic to expect to be hired as a clerk. The owner may not be able to afford another clerk, or he or she may prefer to hire someone older. However, there might be other things you can do, so try to think of what kind of help the owner might need—even before the owner does! "I could run errands for you." "I could make deliveries to the senior citizens' home on the other end of town—I have a bike." "I could come in on the weekends and help you clean up." You might come up with an idea that the owner never thought of, but which he or she likes very much as soon as you make the suggestion.

You and Your Employer: What Each of You Owes the Other

Whether you are working for a big company, a small business, or a private individual (such as the parent of a child you're caring for), when you agree to work for someone else, you are making a contract with that person. You have certain rights and responsibilities, and so does your employer. Before you take a job, it's important to know what will be expected of you—and what you can expect from your employer. That way, you will be in a better position to make the decisions about the job that are right for you.

What Your Employer Expects from You

Every job has its own requirements, of course. But most employers share certain basic expectations. Most businesses require their employees to be on time. They also expect that an employee will show up ready for work— that is, dressed in the appropriate clothes or uniform, awake and alert, rather than tired, hung over, or so distracted that it takes several minutes to actually start working.

In the same vein, most employers expect that workers will restrict or limit entirely the contact they have with friends while they are working. Different employers have different rules about this. If you are babysitting, for example, your clients probably don't want you to have friends over. They have hired you to take care of their child, and that's where they'd like your attention to be. Different people have different rules about this, however, so check it out.

On the other hand, if you are working as a waiter or waitress, the restaurant owner may be happy if your friends come in and order something—as long as you aren't giving more attention to your friends than to the other customers. Again, this is something to check out with your boss.

Certainly, a basic job requirement is that an employee find ways to get along with coworkers, supervisors, and customers. This doesn't mean that you should submit quietly if you are being treated badly. It does mean that most employers are more interested in how their businesses are doing than in anything else. If someone has to make compromises, they usually expect that someone to be their employee, not themselves or their customers. Of course, it's up to you to decide what compromises you're willing to make and where it's important to take a stand.

Likewise, employers expect that you will do the job you were hired to do, no matter what it takes. Again, most employers are more interested in how their businesses are doing than in anything else. If you have a paper route, the newspaper company wants to know that its papers are being delivered—it doesn't want to know why you couldn't do it. If you're working in a store, the store manager wants to know that every customer got waited on quickly—he or she doesn't want to know why some customers got tired of waiting and left.

This expectation of employers can often be quite frustrating. Sometimes on a job, you'll find yourself expected to do something that seems difficult, or impossible. If 20 customers come into a store at once, how are you supposed to wait on all of them? If your bike develops two flat tires at the last minute and there's a pouring rainstorm and you're late for school, how are you supposed to deliver the papers? What about employers who give you far too much work or who give you two jobs to do at once?

Again, you'll have to decide for yourself where you're willing to compromise, where you have room to negotiate, where you can get support from your coworkers, and when the job just isn't worth it anymore. But it will be easier to make those decisions if you understand that your employer's point of view is usually pretty simple: he or she just wants you to get the job done.

What You Can Expect from Your Employer

What about you? What about your requirements? First and foremost, you should be able to expect that you'll get paid the amount that you agreed on, at the time that you agreed on. Usually, the main reason that you have taken a job is because you want the money! If your employer isn't giving it to you, or isn't giving it to you on time, you have a right to complain. If the problem continues, you may want to leave the job. You might also want to take some action to get the money that is owed by you, by contacting your local Department of Labor or Better Business Bureau.

Of course, if your employer is a private individual, such as someone you've babysat for or mowed the lawn for, you probably can't take legal action. Perhaps in that case, you can find some other way to press that person for your money. Or you may have to just consider the loss "a learning experience."

You should also expect that you'll be treated with dignity and respect. When you take a job, you are agreeing that your employer can ask you to do certain things that are part of your job. You may even be agreeing that your employer can give you orders and make criticisms of how you are doing the work. You are not agreeing that your employer can talk to you in insulting terms, use racial or sexual slurs, or humiliate you in front of others. If you are being treated in this way, you'll have to consider whether there's anything you can do alone or with others to stop that treatment—but you should be aware that such treatment goes beyond what an employer should be allowed to do.

You should also expect to be free from unwanted sexual advances. Again, when you take a job, you're agreeing to perform certain tasks, such as taking care of a child or serving food to customers. You are not agreeing to date anyone or to listen to remarks about your private life. Being forced to receive these advances is known as *sexual harassment.*

Under federal law, an employer is not only responsible for his or her own behavior in this regard; he or she must also guarantee you a safe working environment. In other words, if you're a waitress, and customers are insisting that you go out with them or are asking insulting questions, you have a right to expect your boss to intervene. Accepting such treatment is *not* "just part of the job."

If your employer is a family friend or neighbor, such as someone you babysit for or do odd jobs for, you still have the right to be free from unwanted actions or remarks. In such a case, you might seriously consider whether it is a good idea to continue working in such an environment at all.

Sometimes employers in this situation blame the person they're harassing. They say, "Well, how do you expect me to act if you come to work dressed like that?" or "If you let me give you a ride home, what was I supposed to think?" It's important for you to know that nothing you do excuses sexual harassment on their part. Even if your behavior has been inappropriate, theirs should not be. It's perfectly appropriate for an employer to ask you to dress differently or to send you home in a taxi. It's not appropriate for an employer to assume, ever, that hiring you for a job includes the right to intrude on your private life.

The most important thing to remember about your rights and responsibilities on the job is that in the end, it's up to you to decide how to handle them. Working out relationships with employers is one of the most difficult and challenging parts of being an adult, as you may have noticed when you saw your parents or other family members coming home from a hard or frustrating day on the job. Deciding what is and isn't worth it to you, which compromises you're willing to make and which you're not, knowing when you should choose to stand up and argue for what you believe in and when you should choose to bite your tongue in order to keep the peace—all of these are difficult decisions even for people with years of work experience. Learning how to handle these circumstances and what your own values are can only make things easier for you as you continue to be a part of the adult working world.

Other Ways of Earning Money

What if you want to earn money but it's not practical for you to get hired by a regular business? Then it's time to be creative.

First, think of all the people you know and all the people you come in contact with throughout your day and your week. Keep in mind both adults and teenagers. Think of what their lives are like. Think of what they need. Think of what they might be willing to pay somebody to do.

The obvious things you might come up with include types of work we've already talked about: babysitting, yard work, housecleaning, acting as a "mother's helper" (doing some combination of babysitting, housework, errands, and other chores). What about some less obvious things?

A woman in New York City figured out that there were lots of things people had to do that they didn't want to spend their own time on. She established a business that charges an hourly rate for doing these frustrating little chores. For example, she will stand in line to get people the forms they need to apply for a driver's license, take their pets to the vet, or call around to help them find a good babysitter. What things can you think of that you might do that people you know might be willing to pay to have done? Dog-walking? Changing a cat's litter box? Errands? Mending clothes? Help with one or two especially awful household chores, like cleaning the oven or clearing out the basement?

Besides thinking of what you can *do* for others, you might think of what you can *make* for others. Do you cook, sew, work in wood, or do other crafts? Might neighbors, friends, or a local store be interested in what you make? What about your talents: Do you like to write or draw? How about starting a neighborhood magazine that you could print up on a home computer and sell? Could you write personalized poems for special occasions like birthdays and anniversaries? Could you make greeting cards, personalized T-shirts, specially designed stationery? Musicians, do you know people who might want music at a wedding, bar or bas mitzvah, or anniversary party? How about people who might want you to compose a special song for a special occasion?

If making money in these ways appeals to you, try brainstorming to come up with some creative ideas. First, make a list of all the people you know. Make up the list as quickly as possible—don't think about it, just list one name after another, all on one sheet of paper if possible. Then, keeping that piece of paper in front of you, take another sheet of paper and, as quickly as possible, write down all the things you can think of that these people might want. Write down services—help with housework, someone to walk the dog, a person to run errands—as well as products—a great dessert, a special poem, personalized stationery. Again, don't think too hard, just let your imagination play. Finally, on a third sheet of paper, write down everything—literally *everything*—that you know how to do. Don't leave anything out. Include ordinary things like "cooking" and "cleaning out a litter box" as well as more unusual talents like writing or drawing.

If, after making these three lists, you don't find yourself getting a good idea for earning money, don't despair. Put the lists away for a day or two and let your unconscious mind work on the problem. If at the end of the week you still haven't come up with anything, go back and look at your lists again. Picture the people you know going through their daily routines. See them doing their chores, meeting their friends, spending time with their families. Then ask yourself how you can fit into the picture.

Once you come up with a product or service that you could sell, your next step is to explore your idea further, to make sure it will work and that it will be worth it to you. If it takes you six hours to make a piece of handmade stationery and people will only pay 50 cents for it, obviously that's not a good way of earning money. Figure out how many hours you'll be working—and whether you are willing or able to take that time away from your schoolwork, chores at home, and free time. Also figure out how much you'll have to spend on materials—ingredients for baked goods, paper and pencils for artwork, xeroxing for a local newsletter. Make sure that you've got the money to lay out, and check to be sure that you've got a reasonable chance of earning that money back. You might ask around to find out just how much people would be willing to pay for the goods or services you're planning to offer, before actually committing too much time or money to the idea.

If you've checked everything out and you think your idea will fly, your next step is to spread the word. Tell everyone you know what you're selling and ask them to tell everything *they* know. Put up ads in every free place you can find, such as bulletin boards and neighborhood lampposts. (Sometimes you have to get permission to put an ad on a bulletin board, and in some places, it's illegal to post flyers on a lamppost, so check these things out before you do it.) Find out if your local newspaper runs free community service ads and see if you qualify. Keep being creative as you think of ways to let people know what you have to offer.

If your idea works, you will in effect have started your own business. Every businessperson knows that running a business can be difficult, time-consuming, expensive, and disappointing. Prices that were just right when you started might turn out to be too high. Demand that started out strong might fall off. Something you thought could be done quickly and easily may take much more time than you had counted on. Sometimes customers don't pay you, or don't pay you on time.

On the other hand, starting your own business can be quite rewarding, both emotionally and financially. If you look on the whole process as a learning experience, one in which you're taking risks that might or might not pay off, you'll be in a good position to enjoy the good aspects and handle the bad aspects efficiently. And you'll have the satisfaction of knowing that you've developed your own qualities of responsibility, perseverance, resourcefulness, and initiative. Whether your project goes just the way you'd like it to or not, these are valuable qualities that will serve you well in the world of work and money.

5

How to Save Money and Spend It Wisely: Budgets and Other Helpful Hints

Whether you are earning money, receiving an allowance, or both, you may not feel that you have as much money as you would like. One way of making your money go further is to make a *budget*—a plan of how to spend and save your money.

A budget usually has two halves—a record of the money that you receive and a plan for how to spend it. Many budgets include plans for saving, as well. Here is an example of a very simple budget:

SANDY'S BASIC BUDGET

Money Coming in Every Week   **Expenses**
Allowance—$5.00   Bus fare—$3.00
Babysitting—$15.00   School supplies—$5.00
Total—$20.00   Total—$8.00

Total money minus total expenses:
$20.00 – $8.00 = $12.00

$12.00 a week to divide between spending and saving
Movies: $5.00/week
Snacks: $5.00/week
Savings: $2.00/week

Many people have never made a budget. The idea of making a budget feels too restrictive or upsetting, because it means facing the reality that we don't always have all the money we would like and that there may be some things that we cannot buy or cannot afford.

Other people make budget after budget but never manage to stick to the plans they make for themselves. Making a budget may feel soothing—a way of promising themselves that they can solve their money problems—but in actual fact, their budgets don't help them to spend money in more satisfying ways.

Still other people make budgets that just don't work. These people make what seems like a realistic plan, and they stick to it—but somehow they still end up short of money or in financial trouble.

As we've seen in the previous chapters, money is a complicated issue. Many emotions and messages are tied up in money, beyond the practical questions of how much we receive and how much we spend. Naturally, these emotional issues get involved in budget-making, as well. However, sometimes people's difficulties with budgets do come only from practical problems.

In this chapter, we'll start by talking about budgets and saving money in very practical terms. If you find this discussion helpful in making your budget, congratulations! You're on your way to spending and saving your money in ways that feel comfortable and satisfying to you. But if you feel frustrated, anxious, or upset, read on. In the second half of the chapter, we'll go on to discuss some of the emotional issues that frequently come up around spending, saving, and having money.

Secrets of a Successful Budget

Here are three secrets to a successful budget:

1. *Start from the most conservative version of reality that you know.* If you know you get an allowance of five dollars every week, but sometimes your parents give you an extra dollar or so, does that extra dollar belong in your budget? Not really. As long as you don't know for sure that the extra money is coming in, it's better not to count on it. That way, if the money doesn't come in, you don't have to change your spending and savings plan. If it does come in, you can enjoy your extra money.

Of course, some extras *can* be counted on. If your Aunt Martha has given you 10 dollars for your birthday ever since you were two, you can probably figure a once-a-year 10 dollars into your budget. If your parents are irregular in *when* they give you extra money, but do in fact give you at least five extra dollars a month, you can put down those five extra dollars. Just be sure you are working with the "*bottom line*"—the money you *know* you can count on.

2. *Be realistic about what you are going to spend.* Let's say that you decide to save money by riding your bike to after-school sports instead of taking the bus. You figure that

at 50 cents a bus ride, six bus rides a week, you've saved three dollars a week. So far, so good. But what about the days when it's raining? Will you still be willing to take your bike, or are you going to want to "splurge" on the bus? What about the day your friend says, "Come home on the bus with me and we can have dinner at my house"? Are you going to say, "You take the bus and I'll meet you"? If you know yourself and your habits, be realistic. Figure that you'll save *some* money by not taking the bus, but budget in one or two bus trips a week, just to be on the safe side.

3. *Think about the future as well as about the present.* One of the great things about a budget is that it gives you control over your money and your spending in the long term as well as in the short term. And one of the rewards that makes it worthwhile sticking to a budget is that it helps you find ways to save up for things you otherwise couldn't afford.

A successful budget might have two sections: immediate expenses and long-term goals. Immediate expenses are things that you need right away, every day. Items like bus fare, club dues, and school supplies are immediate expenses—costs you must pay within a short amount of time, purchases that you can't put off.

Immediate expenses might also include the money you have to spend for fun. If you want to go to one movie a week, the movie ticket should go into your budget as an immediate expense. If you can't get through the day without buying yourself a treat at the local store, put down your "treat money" as an immediate expense.

When you've added up your immediate expenses, you can see how they compare with the money you have coming in. If you have some money left over, you can decide on what you want to do with it. If you have no money left over, or if your immediate expenses are more than the money coming in, you can see that you have a problem. You'll either have to find a way to get more money or cut down on your immediate expenses.

You might also be motivated either to earn more or to cut back on expenses when you identify some of the long-term goals you might want to save up for. Here are some items that people might put down for long-term goals:

- $75.00 for a new leather jacket
- $100.00 for a new tape deck
- $25.00 for a summer trip to the State Fair
- As much money as possible in a savings account for a long trip I'd like to take someday

Once you know what you'd do with more money if you had it, you can decide whether or not saving up for your goals is worth it to you. You'll have to balance how important your immediate expenses are against how much you want to save for the future. Either way, a budget can help you see the problem clearly, so you can decide how you want to handle it.

On the following page is an example of a budget that takes all of these principles into account. As you can see, it's a more complicated budget than the one shown earlier in the chapter because it includes more information about the person's money and plans.

As you can see, Pat divided the money coming in into two categories—money that definitely came in every week, and money that usually came in over the course of a month. One of her babysitting jobs, at the Browns, was a regular job every Thursday night—the Browns' bowling night. The rest of her babysitting money was a little more uncertain. Sometimes she got babysitting jobs on the weekend, but sometimes she didn't. Pat thought hard about whether she wanted to plan to do more babysitting in order to earn more money, or whether she wanted to be free sometimes on weekend nights to do things with her friends. She decided that her free time was more important to her than the extra money, and

---

PAT'S BUDGET

Money Usually Coming in Every Month

Every Week	*Sometimes*
Allowance—$5.00	Babysitting—$15.00 each week
Babysitting—$10.00	(Parents' extras—$10.00 each month)
	~~(Birthday money—$25.00 each year)~~
Total—$15.00	Total—$70.00 each month

Immediate Expenses—Every Week
$4.00 bus fare
$6.00 movie
$5.00 snacks
Total—$15.00   Total income every week: $15.00
$15.00 – $15.00 = 0

Immediate Expenses—Every Month
$5.00—camera club dues
$20.00—things to buy at the mall
$20.00—CDs, records, and cassettes
Total—$45.00   Money that usually comes in: $70.00
$70.00 – $45.00 = $25.00

I will save the $25.00 left over every month. At the end of a year I'll have $300, which I'll use to buy a special camera.

---

she didn't want to plan to babysit both nights every weekend—only some weekends.

So Pat decided to use the money that definitely came in every week to meet her immediate expenses each week. The money that usually came in she used for more flexible expenses over the course of the month—buying jewelry, cosmetics, CDs, and cassettes. Pat wanted to be sure she had enough money to see a movie and buy snacks every week but felt that if she was short of money, she wouldn't mind waiting a week or so to buy a special CD. She also used her "usually comes in" money to save for her long-term goals.

That way, if less money came in than she expected, she might save a little more slowly, but she didn't have to worry about running out of money for the things she really needed or wanted each week.

As you can see, Pat started out by putting her birthday money into her budget and then crossed it out. She decided that it wasn't sensible to budget money that came in only once a year. When the money came in, she would decide either to buy herself a special treat or to save it, but she wouldn't make that money part of her regular plan.

Making Your Own Budget

Do you want to try making your own budget? You can use the budgets in this chapter as models. Here are some other hints on how to get started:

1. Make a list of all the money that you definitely receive every week. Total it up and label the total "Money coming in every week."

2. Now make a list of any other money that comes in over the course of a month. If you're not sure how much is coming in, choose the lowest possible figure—you'll enjoy spending the extra money if it comes in, but you won't have counted on it. Total up this second list and label it, "Money usually coming in every month."

3. Next, make a list of money that you definitely spend every week. Again, be realistic. If you plan to give up certain things to save money, ask yourself if you will really be able to give them up. If you plan on going to a movie, for example, but not buying a snack, make sure that you really mean to follow this plan. Perhaps you make this resolution but then find that you're always saying "just this once." Or perhaps you keep to your resolution but find that you don't enjoy movies nearly as

much if you can't munch on popcorn while you watch them. Be good to yourself! A budget is not supposed to make you miserable—it's supposed to help you figure out how to enjoy the money that you do have.

Once you've totaled up your weekly expenses, you may find that they are greater than your weekly income. In that case, you'll have to figure out a solution. Can you use *some* of the money that comes in every month to cover your weekly expenses? Is there a way to cut back that you haven't thought of? Is there a way you could earn more money?

4.   Before you answer these questions, however, continue making a list of the expenses that come up over the month. Total these and label them "Monthly expenses."

5.   Now you can compare all four types of money—the money that comes in every week, the money that comes in over the month, the money that must go out every week, and the money that you want to spend over the month. You can play around with these figures until you get them to work for you. You might need to cut expenses, but you might just need to rearrange them a little. For example, you might decide that you can buy a snack at the movies on the weeks when you have an extra babysitting or yard work job, but not on the weeks when you don't. Or you might decide that if you bought only one CD a month instead of the three you now buy, you could use the leftover money to pay for snacks at the movies.

6.   Once you've figured out how to balance your expenses against your income, make a list of things you'd like to save up for and label it "Long-term Goals." Then look long and hard at that list. How much do you want the things that are on it? Badly enough to give up some of the things that you are now spending money on every week or every month? Badly enough to take on more jobs or find another way of earning money? Listing your goals and comparing them to where you are now is an excellent

way to help yourself make decisions. It's a way of deciding on what you really want and how much you are willing to sacrifice in order to get it.

When Budgets Just Don't Seem to Work

We've talked about how to make a successful budget that will help you balance your spending and saving—but what if you've followed all the suggestions and you're still not sticking to your budget? Don't worry—you're not alone! Here are just some of the ways that people act when they have trouble following their budgets:

- At the beginning of the week or month they give themselves just "one thing extra," promising to cut back on something else to make it up by the end of the week or month—but somehow that never happens. "Just one thing extra" keeps adding up until the budget is history.
- They stick faithfully to their budget almost to the end of the week or month—and then blow it on one big item that they just "had to have."
- They keep finding expenses that weren't in the budget, so the budget just doesn't work.
- They stick to their budget for a few weeks or months at a time, then feel so frustrated by how little they can spend that they just give up.

Sometimes these budget problems are practical problems. If you're finding expenses you didn't expect, you can go back and rewrite your budget to include them. If you're frustrated with how little money your budget allows you to spend, you might want to rewrite it to allow yourself more money for treats—or you might decide you need to earn more money so that you can afford the things you want.

Sometimes, though, budget problems reflect deeper feelings about money. If you feel that your friends won't like you or that people won't want to date you unless you spend more money, then of course you'll have a powerful reason to ignore the good planning you've done in your budget. If you feel that the only or the best way you can be good to yourself is to buy yourself a treat, then of course having the treat is going to feel more important to you than sticking to your budget.

These are not bad feelings—but they may be feelings that are getting in your way. Sometimes just recognizing these feelings can be enough to help you put them aside. Just saying, "People will love me for myself, not for the clothes I own, the money I spend, or the treats I buy them," can sometimes be enough to help you get clear of feeling bad. Making a list of all the treats you can give yourself that cost little or no money—a bubble bath, a quiet evening in your room, a long talk with a friend, a walk in the park—might be enough to help you change your spending and treating patterns.

If you feel that the problems go deeper, however, you might want to take more action. Talk to a friend, a sympathetic adult, or a school counselor. Call a hot line or look in the telephone book for a social service agency that offers counseling. (Some resources are listed in Chapter 7 of this book.) Many people find that it helps to talk to a sympathetic, understanding person about their feelings of pain and fear. If you think that feelings about money are keeping you from enjoying your life as much as you could, you might find it useful to get help in dealing with those feelings.

Saving Your Money

Once your budget is in place, you may find yourself with extra money. You may be saving this money toward a particular goal or simply enjoying the feeling of putting money away with the idea of buying something later. Either way, where do you keep the money you've saved?

If you're dealing with a relatively small amount, say, under $100, it might be appropriate to keep the money at home. A piggy bank, a money box, a special hiding place in a desk or dresser drawer, or some other private place could be a good place to keep your savings. However, be sure that you really have chosen a safe and secure place.

Even if you are only saving a few dollars at a time, you might want to put your money into a savings account in a bank. Certainly you will want to follow this option if your savings grow to $100 or more.

A *savings account* is an arrangement that a bank makes with you to hold your money until you need it. A checking account allows you to use your money to buy things or pay debts to other people, simply by writing a check. Unlike a checking account, a savings account does not usually allow you access to your money unless you actually go to the bank and withdraw the money. (However, some savings accounts come with plastic cash cards that can be used to withdraw money from cash machines.) Not being able to get at their money too easily helps some people to save.

Another advantage of a savings account is that it pays interest. Every month, you will receive a small percentage of the money that remains in the account. The interest on a savings account is what the bank pays you for the use of your money. While your money is in the bank, it is being lent to other bank customers who are taking out loans or it is invested in businesses in which the bank is involved. The bank is charging interest on those loans, or receiving dividends on its investments. Some of that money finds its way back to you, in the form of interest on your account.

Sometimes banks have strict rules about savings accounts. You may not be allowed to withdraw any money for 30 days after you make your first deposit. Or there may be some penalties for withdrawing too much money too fast. If you do open a savings account, make sure you have found out all the rules and restrictions before depositing your money.

Most banks will not accept savings accounts from people under 18 without the signature of a parent or a guardian. This means that technically, your parent or guardian is also authorized to withdraw money from your account. However, no one else besides them is allowed to take money from your savings account. When you want to withdraw your money, you yourself will probably be required to present a *passbook*—a book with a record of your account— or a *withdrawal slip*—a form with your account number. Once again, the bank may require a parent or guardian's permission or co-signature if you wish to withdraw money or close your account.

A Word About Credit Cards

Many people these days have credit cards—pieces of plastic that stores and restaurants will accept in place of money. When a store accepts a credit card, it bills the credit card company instead of you. Then the credit card company sends *you* a bill. However, on most credit cards, you don't have to pay the entire bill right away. You can pay the bill off in *installments*, or sections. Usually, the credit card company will require a minimum payment each month, although you have the option of paying more. In effect, the credit card company is lending you the money to make your purchases.

The catch is that the company charges *interest*—a fee—for lending you that money. Most credit card companies charge from 16 percent to 19 percent interest annually, which can add up to over 50 dollars in one year on only a few hundred dollars' worth of charges.

The other catch is that if you buy things that you can't afford at the time, you might not be able to afford them later on, either. While credit cards can be a useful way of putting off expenses until you have more income, they can also be a trap that encourages people to take on too much debt and buy things they can't afford.

If you've been having difficulty with a family credit card, take the advice of most budget planners: Never use credit cards to make daily purchases—use them only for special expenses; and never use a credit card to buy something unless you know *exactly* when and where the money is coming from to pay off the card.

And of course, remember—if you can't pay off a credit card bill right away, you wind up paying even more money than your original purchase! Practice in using credit cards with caution now will pay off in good budget practices when you are an adult with credit cards of your own.

6

Money and
Families

No matter how you have decided to come to terms with money, the major source of money and financial decision-making in your life right now is not you, but your parents or guardians. Unless you are living in very unusual circumstances, you are probably being supported and cared for in some way by an adult who has the ultimate decision-making power over how much money you receive, whether and how much you can work, and what happens to the money you earn.

Even if your parents give you a regular allowance and complete freedom in your earning and spending habits, their feelings and decisions about money are going to have a major impact on your life. If they are having financial problems, you will feel the impact. If they are concerned about money, you will probably be aware of their worry, even if they take care never to discuss financial matters with you.

It can be frustrating to recognize that your parents' feelings about money are so powerful in *your* life, especially when you can't change the basic structure of the situation until you're 18 or on your own. However, recognizing the importance of your parents' feelings about money is the first step toward dealing with your own feelings about how they act. Once you're aware both of how your parents are affecting you and how you feel about it, you may be able to take action, with yourself, with them, or both, to improve communication and possibly to change your situation.

Money Pressures

Here are some of the money pressures that your parents may be under. As you can see, some of these pressures are problems that come from the outside world and some come more from people's feelings about money and the messages they have received about it. All of these pressures feel equally real to the person undergoing them, however—and all may be affecting your parents' attitude and behavior.

- Fear of losing a job.
- Frustration with a dull or unpleasant job, but feeling that no other job that pays well enough is available.
- Fear of a plant closing, with the consequent unemployment, business problems, and so on.
- Fear of losing a business or doing badly in a business.
- Anxiety about not having enough money. This could include anything from fear of losing a home or being evicted to frustration at not being able to buy the latest-model car or the most fashionable clothes.
- Guilt over not providing a better life for their children. Believe it or not, some parents think that they have failed as parents if they can't give their kids everything the kids want—or everything that the neighbors' kids have.
- Guilt over not being able to provide more help to relatives in need.

- Jealousy of another family member who is better off financially.
- Worries about financial security in old age.
- Worries about paying medical bills, either current bills or bills resulting from a possible future catastrophe.
- Frustration at not being able to save enough to make a special purchase.
- Anxiety about being in debt, through credit cards, personal loans, or mortgages (loans taken out with a house or a piece of property as security. If the loan isn't paid back on time, the house or property goes to the bank to cover the loan.).
- Feeling like a failure for not having more money.

Can you think of other pressures that your parents might be feeling about money?

These pressures may be expressed in a variety of ways. For example, perhaps every time you mention money, one of your parents blows up. He or she seems to be constantly angry about the whole topic of money, so that everything you say triggers an explosion.

Or, maybe your parents make constant worried references to money, money problems, and the terrible things that may happen without enough money. A parent might say, "I don't know what's going to happen—we'll probably end up in the street!" or "If this keeps up, we'll all have to go on welfare." You may already have figured out that these terrible things never quite happen—but it's also difficult to tell just how serious the problems are. Perhaps one day they *will* happen—from the way your parents talk about it, you just can't tell.

Some people express their own anxieties about money by making belittling references to other people, either because they have money or because they don't. For example, "I don't know what she's got to complain about, she's doing all right for herself," or "He has no right to have an opinion on anything—have you seen that horrible old car he drives?" These belittling references may extend to you. Perhaps one or both parents mock your job or your own efforts to live on a budget.

Perhaps they criticize you for spending too much—or too little. Whether your parents criticize you directly or not, you may feel that money and spending are very dangerous topics because the possibility is always there that they will be grounds for humiliation.

Other parents display grudging attitudes about money. Say you do your chores and you're supposed to get an allowance in return—but your parents act as though they're doing you an enormous favor which they might withhold at any time. You find this confusing—after all, if they don't want to give you an allowance, why are they doing it? You thought you had a deal—chores in exchange for allowance—but now your parents seem to think they're doing you a favor. You get the message that money is something that you can never earn or count on; it's always something to be given on a whim.

One of the most frustrating responses can be parents' inconsistent attitudes about money. Perhaps your parents are sometimes generous, sometimes grudging. Sometimes they are confident and enjoy spending money; other times they are paralyzed with fear and anxiety. In this case, you may get the message that money is something dangerous and mysterious—that it isn't possible to have an understandable, logical relationship to it.

If any of these ideas sound familiar, take heart. As we've seen throughout this book, most people have emotional attitudes regarding money, and why should the people in your family be the exceptions? The problem comes not when people have emotional attitudes about money, but when these attitudes get in the way of good communication and good relationships.

Opening the Lines of Communication

If you feel upset about your parents' attitudes about money, the first step is to identify in yourself what is bothering you. Try putting the following words at the top of an empty page: *"I'm upset about money be-cause . . . ."* Then fill in the rest of the page with what-ever comes to mind, writing quickly, without stopping to think. You might surprise yourself by what you write!

You might also write at the top of a page, *"I'm upset about my parents' attitudes toward money because . . . ."* Once again, you may learn some interesting things about your thoughts and feelings.

Of course, these pages are for your eyes only. If you are going to explore your thoughts and feelings freely, you have to know that you are doing so in privacy. Later you can decide what you want to tell your parents and how you want to phrase it. For now, just let it all out.

Once you have gotten in touch with what's bothering you, you may want to talk about it with your parents. In these kinds of conversations, it's most helpful to avoid blame. Instead, just say what you feel and what you would like to have happen, and then ask the other person what he or she would like to do. Here are some ways you might start such a conversation:

"I've heard you talk a lot lately about how bad our money situation is. You've said we're going to end up on the street, which really scares me. Is that true? I'd really like to know whether we're in an emergency or not."

"Every time you give me my allowance, you make some remark about how I don't really deserve it. I feel terrible when that happens."

"Whenever I buy something with my own money, you make some kind of criticism. I feel like you don't trust me to handle my own money. I'd really like to have the chance to buy things for myself and see what happens, even if I do make mistakes sometimes."

Negotiating with Parents About Money

Sometimes the best way to deal with parents in money issues is to stick to the practical side of the problem. Maybe you can work out specific ways of handling money issues in ways that ease the strain surrounding this topic. Here are some issues that you may want to negotiate:

- the size of your allowance
- what you are supposed to do in exchange for your allowance
- whether or not you get your allowance on time
- whether your allowance gets suspended or reduced if you haven't done your chores or haven't done them on time
- whether there is any other reason that your allowance can be suspended
- what, if any, restrictions there are on what you can buy with your own money, whether it's an allowance or money you've earned some other way
- how you can act responsibly toward family finances

Negotiations are a process of give and take. You may find it helpful to think about the give and take of your relationship with your parents concerning money. For example, if you are frustrated by the small size of your allowance, perhaps you could offer to do more chores in exchange for getting more money. If your parents are irregular about when they give you your allowance, perhaps you could make a deal: you'll do your chores on time if they will give you your allowance on time. If your parents use suspending your allowance as punishment and you find that especially frustrating, perhaps you could work out other ways of punishment that involve doing more chores or substituting other restrictions, rather than money.

One thing that can help in negotiations with parents is keeping their point of view in mind. Do they have particular worries about you and money? Address those worries to reassure them:

"I know you're worried about my learning to handle money responsibly, but now is the time for me to make my own mistakes—while I'm still living with you!"

"If you're worried about my not doing my chores on time, maybe we could make a chart. I could check off when the chores are done, so you wouldn't have to nag and I wouldn't feel like you were always waiting for me to screw up."

"If I promise to do my schoolwork and to keep my grades up, will that make it easier for you to give me permission to take this job?"

When Problems Can't Be Solved Alone

Sometimes families have problems with money that go beyond a teenager's or pre-teen's ability to negotiate. If you recognize any of these problems in your family, we urge you to go outside your family to get help. Talk to a school counselor or another sympathetic adult. Call a hot line or find a counseling agency in the phone book or see those agencies listed in Chapter 7. However you do it, find someone to share your problem and help you find a solution. These are some of the money problems families may need help with.

Compulsive Gambling

Many people enjoy an occasional evening of gambling, whether it's a weekly poker night or a weekend trip to Las Vegas. However, if a member of your family is a compulsive gambler, that means that he or she has a problem with gambling that is out of control. If basic family expenses like food, clothing, and rent are suffering from this person's gambling, or if the family is continually giving up treats and extras to pay for a gambling habit, then there is a problem.

Compulsive Spending

Some people handle frustrations and worries by drinking too much, eating too much, or smoking too much. Other people handle these problems by spending too much.

Compulsive spenders don't simply enjoy an occasional trip to a store when they're feeling blue. They buy *compulsively*—in a way that seems to be out of their control. They may buy several pairs of shoes at once, for example, and never even take them out of the box. Or they may run up huge debts on credit cards for things they really don't need. A compulsive spender might spend money that had been set aside for the phone bill on a new outfit or a new appliance—and then watch in bewilderment when the phone is turned off.

If someone in your family is a compulsive spender, this is a serious problem that is affecting your welfare. You have the right to get help in solving this problem.

Compulsive Hoarding

Just as some people compulsively spend, others compulsively *hoard*, or save. Some hoarding may be natural, as when a person saves a huge stack of newspapers or magazines, saying, "I'll get around to reading these some day." But again, compulsive hoarding goes beyond this normal behavior to a point where the hoarding is actively interfering with family life. In extreme cases, whole rooms may be filled with items that the hoarder has saved. Or the hoarder may be afraid to spend money, even on necessities like a visit to the doctor.

Neglect

Some money problems come out in neglect of the children in a family. When we say neglect, we don't mean that you haven't got as large an allowance as you'd like or that you can't always afford the latest clothing styles. We mean that you're not getting proper food, or that the clothing you own is wildly inappropriate for someone of your age and sex, or that you don't have basic necessities like a warm winter coat or regular doctor visits.

If you are experiencing neglect, once again, we urge you to tell someone and get help. You have a right to good care, and you have the right to take action to get it.

You and Money: An Ongoing Relationship

Developing satisfying attitudes toward getting, spending, and saving money is a lifelong process. People's attitudes toward money often change as they get older and their situations change. As you continue to mature, you will continue to have responsibilities and concerns involving money. You'll have decisions to make about jobs, spending, and your future education and career. You'll learn more about your family's financial situation and get a fuller sense of the money problems faced by your parents. You'll come in contact with a wider range of people, and consequently, with a wider range of attitudes toward money—as well as a wider range of incomes.

You will also gain a greater sense of freedom and power where money is concerned. The older you get, the more likely you are to be earning part or all of your own money—and enjoying the freedom that goes with it! Meanwhile, keep thinking about the ways you feel most comfortable spending, saving, and earning money. The thinking you do about money now will not only help you face tough issues now—it will give you a good head start for later on.

7

Where to Find More Information

The following agencies provide information to individuals and groups about personal and institutional money matters.

Budget and Credit Counseling Services
55 Fifth Avenue
New York, NY 10003
212-675-5070
Provides information and referrals to consumers interested in restructuring their personal debt

Bureau of the Mint
Department of the Treasury
501 13th Street NW
Washington, DC 20220
202-376-0837
Provides current and historical information on coins, medals, and currency

Chamber of Commerce of the United States
1615 H Street NW
Washington, DC   20062
202-659-6000
Answers inquiries and makes referrals on matters of business and education in consumer affairs, among other areas

Comptroller of the Currency
Department of the Treasury
490 L'Enfant Plaza East
Washington, DC   20219
202-447-1810
Answers inquiries and provides information on U.S. banking laws

Debtors Anonymous
212-969-0710 (NY state)
212-642-8222 (national meeting hot line)
This organization provides support and referrals to those whose lives have become unmanageable because of debt.

Department of Commerce
14th Street and Constitution Avenue NW
Washington, DC   20230
202-377-2000
Provides free information on U.S. economic development

Federal Deposit Insurance Corporation
550 17th Street NW
Washington, DC   20429
202-389-4221
Provides information regarding the safeguarding of the nation's money supply

Gam-Anon
212-903-4200
This organization provides support to families of compulsive gamblers.

Gamblers Anonymous
445 West 45th Street
New York, NY 10036
212-265-8600
This organization provides support to those who are compulsive gamblers.

Internal Revenue Service
Public Affairs Division
1111 Constitution Avenue NW
Room 1111
Washington, DC 20224
202-566-4045
Provides information on the tax laws of the U.S.

International Numismatic Society
P.O. Box 66555
Washington, DC 20035
202-223-4497
Coordinates worldwide numismatic (coin-related) research

National Council on Compulsive Gambling
445 West 59th Street
Room 1521
New York, NY 10019
212-765-3833
This organization provides referrals to compulsive gamblers and their families.

National Foundation for Consumer Credit
8701 Georgia Avenue
Suite 507
Silver Spring, MD 20910
1-800-388-2227
301-589-5600
This organization provides budget counseling to consumers with minor or major budget problems. Most states list the

local chapter of this organization under Consumer Credit Counseling (CCC) in the white or yellow pages of the telephone directory.

Spender Menders
Dept. PBO Box 15000-156
San Francisco, CA   94119
This organization provides referrals to those who are seeking to restructure their personal finances.

Treasurer of the United States
Department of the Treasury
15th Street and Pennsylvania Avenue NW
Washington, DC   20220
202-566-2843
Compiles information about history and statistics relating to U.S. currency

INDEX